W9-BKK-137

CHARRED
& SCRUFFED

CHARRED & SCRUFFED

Bold new techniques for explosive flavor
on and off the grill

ADAM PERRY LANG

WITH PETER KAMINSKY

Published by Artisan
A division of Workman Publishing Company, Inc.
225 Varick Street
New York, NY 10014-4381
www.artisanbooks.com

Published simultaneously in Canada by Thomas Allen & Son, Limited

---

Library of Congress Cataloging-in-Publication Data
Perry Lang, Adam.
Charred & scruffed / Adam Perry Lang with Peter Kaminsky.
      p. cm.
Includes index.
ISBN 978-1-57965-465-8
1. Barbecuing. 2. Cookbooks. I. Kaminsky, Peter. II. Title. III. Title:
Charred and scruffed.
TX840.B3P479 2012
641.7'6—dc23   2011031786

Design by Interstate Associates • www.interstateteam.com
Illustrations by Linn Trones

Printed in China
First printing, April 2012

10 9 8 7 6 5 4 3 2 1

This book is dedicated to a chef and a place. The chef is Daniel Boulud, and the place is his restaurant, Daniel. Daniel gave me a foundation on how to approach not only cooking, but also life: work hard, work smart, do your best, never underestimate your abilities, and then work even harder. His passion and drive for our craft is a shining example and a valuable practical lesson. I was lucky to have been part of Daniel's team. The lessons stay with me for a lifetime. Chef, I am grateful.

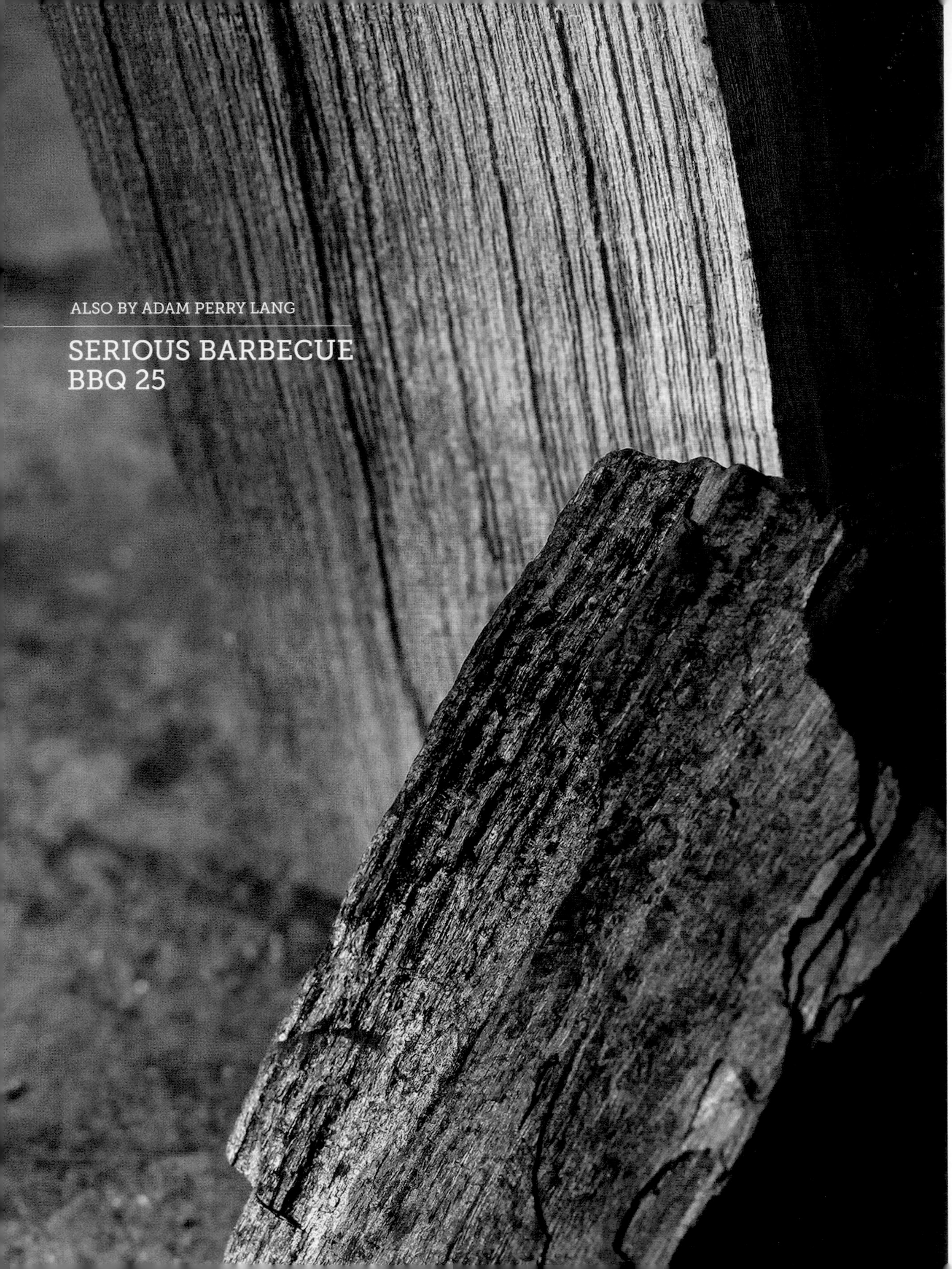

ALSO BY ADAM PERRY LANG

SERIOUS BARBECUE
BBQ 25

CONTENTS

Barbecue: The Next Step *by Peter Kaminsky*   ix
Making Better Barbecue   xiii

Part I: The Theory and Practice of Barbecue   2
Building Explosive Flavor   5
Making Heat Work for You   17

Part II: Meat, Fish, and Fowl   28
Classics Revisited   30
High and Slow   58
Clinching: Down and Dirty   84
Clinched and Planked   106

Part III: Co-Stars   132
Melting, Creamy, and Comfortable   134
Crispy, Fresh, and Sprightly   158
Leaves, Lettuces, and Greens   174
Crispy Bits   194

Part IV: Finishing   206
Spackles   208
Bastes   226
Finishing Salts   240

Sources   256
Index   257

BARBECUE:
THE NEXT STEP

People love barbecue. The combination of fire, smoke, salt, and meat is probably the first recipe that humans ever discovered. Even vegetarians are programmed to love meat prepared this way: they choose not to eat it, which just leaves more for the rest of us.

This is a new and different kind of barbecue book because it is about invention, not tradition. Most collections of barbecue recipes try to help the home grillmaster achieve the same results as a beloved old-time barbecue stand on a little-traveled country road: the kind of place that has a hand-lettered sign promising a plate of satisfying ribs, pulled pork, Brunswick stew, creamed corn, coleslaw, and mac and cheese.

You could think of these classic joints as the food version of folk music: pure, memorable, and unchanging. To continue the folk music analogy, in the 1960s new and original artists— supreme among them, Bob Dylan—added a modern sensibility to the heritage of mountain ballads, delta blues, and field hollers. We've been waiting for someone like that to come along in the world of barbecue: a chef who understands the subtlety of modern gastronomy yet appreciates the pure flavor power of the American barbecue tradition.

Enter Adam Perry Lang.

Rather than simply trying to duplicate the flavor that a blue-ribbon pitmaster learned from his daddy and his granddaddy, Adam Perry Lang has devoted a trained chef's palate and sensibility to answering the question "How can I take this great legacy and make something new out of it?"

Adam was trained in some of the "hautest" haute cuisine restaurants in America and France, but when he felt he had reached the point in his career where he wanted to follow his own path, he turned to the indigenous American barbecue tradition and set out to refine, concentrate, and reassemble the flavors and textures on the barbecue plate.

Like all truly original chefs, he developed his own language of heat, flavor, and technique. Adam is, in his own words, "an active griller." As you will see in this book, when he grills, he treats meat, fish, and poultry like a hot potato, flipping, then instantly basting while the main ingredient is still sizzling and hot. In this way Adam slowly develops a crisp, chewy, savory crust with layer upon layer of flavor.

He is not afraid to fly in the face of the conventional barbecue dogma of "low and slow." For big cuts of meat, he creates a strong fire but then places the meat far away from the coals (see High and Slow, pages 58–83). So, while, for example, Rib Roast Done Like a Steak (page 71) cooks relatively slowly, when its fat and juices hit the coals, they vaporize and flavor the meat in a way that cooking over a low fire never can.

On the other hand, when he cooks "low," he cooks really low, actually placing meat directly on the hot coals so that it crusts immediately and cooks through just as quickly. It was nothing short of a revelation to me to see lamb chops cooked over hot coals yet with absolutely no flame or acrid smoke (see page 102). Your friends and family will not believe this is possible, but when they see you do it, they'll respond the way one does to a masterly magic trick.

A true postmodernist, Adam deconstructs traditional barbecue and then reassembles it to more powerful effect. His Finishing Salts (pages 240–55) add a final touch of direct and powerful flavor just before serving. His Spackles (pages 208–25), which come into play when you top off a forkful of meat, fish, or poultry just before putting it in your mouth, take the place of mustard, ketchup, and mayonnaise but serve the same purpose: a condiment that complements and completes the taste experience.

Be sure to try Adam's recipes for what he calls "Co-Stars" (pages 132–205). Surely, beans, coleslaw, and macaroni salad can't exhaust the list of wonderful foods that can complete a meal that features meat on the fire. His side dishes, far from afterthoughts, provide contrast and synergy with "mains."

This, then, is a book for the fire worshipper in every cook. If you thought the last word had been written on the subject, you are in for a surprise. With *Charred & Scruffed,* the next chapter in barbecue is being written—it's all about good ingredients, wood fire, new recipes, and the technique of a world-class chef.

—Peter Kaminsky

MAKING BETTER BARBECUE

I have always loved barbecue. While I can't claim that my grandpa was a great pitmaster, I can say that in my case, encountering the deep savory smokiness of barbecued meat was love at first whiff. I came to understand that wood fire, seasoning, and smoke combine in a form of culinary alchemy that—in all its strongly defended regional variations—makes up the great tradition of American barbecue. What I have tried to do in my cooking, and in this book, is to apply the lessons of classic cuisine to the folkways of barbecue.

Along the way, I read a lot of barbecue cookbooks, but after the first half dozen or so, what was striking to me was how similar they are. You're sure to find falling-off-the bone ribs, mahogany-hued briskets, manly (i.e., really huge) cuts of steak, and succulent smoked pork shoulders that taste like the distilled essence of Old Dixie. But upon closer reading, and tasting, you may also find that the meat, which is often the most expensive ingredient in the recipe, is relegated to second fiddle for bastes, sauces, spice rubs, and, for good measure, some hot sauce and vinegar at the end.

My aim is to construct a more powerful taste narrative. I always strive to have different layers of flavor and texture come through, one after the other, so that each bite is a story with a beginning, middle, and end. And when the story is told, what should stay with you is the quality of the prime ingredient . . . the meat. Remember this: meat is the master. Sauce, seasoning, and smoke are its faithful servants.

ACTIVE GRILLING

When I first began to study the craft of barbecue, many of the masters I looked to for inspiration made it a point of pride that you didn't worry over your meat. Once you put something on the grill or in the smoker, the time-honored wisdom was that the less you moved it, touched it, or looked in on it, the better it would come out. They would say, "You just got to leave it alone." It was almost as if checking on your steak, chop, or chicken was a sign of personal insecurity that the meat itself could sense and, once it knew about this, it would deliver something dry, tough, and tasteless.

Yes, a lot of people believe you should just put something on the grill and not move it, but I'm not one of those people. I like to flip, baste, and move from the hotter to the cooler parts of the grill, and I do all of this to develop crust and flavor. I'm an active griller. Whenever I am around food and fire, I am always asking myself, What's happening where the heat comes into contact with what is cooking? In a way, I suppose, that means I am into molecular gastronomy. But I don't want to scare you off—I certainly don't mean that I am a fan of the foams and science-project creations that you see on ambitious menus these days. You won't find little spheres of olive oil and squid ink formed in a bath of liquid nitrogen on any of my menus. That kind of deconstruction and reconstruction of food can be very imaginative and, at times, quite nice, but I find that the whole real products—meat, fish, poultry, vegetables—are so complex and nuanced that I don't think I can improve on things by putting them in an atom smasher in hopes that something interesting and delicious will pop out.

Still, I am a molecular kind of guy to the extent that I am constantly thinking of what happens to every molecule of food when it is subjected to heat. I try to visualize what's going on all through the cooking process. How does heat affect the crust? How does it penetrate into the moist inner muscle fibers? How and when does it start the delicate unwrapping of the collagen that allows it to swell and hydrate and give properly cooked meat its mouthwatering unctuousness?

Thinking in this way, imagining that I can almost see what is happening to every meat fiber, guides me through the cooking process, and it lets me adjust and improve as I go. Thinking small produces big results.

Part I

THE THEORY AND PRACTICE OF BARBECUE

I n barbecue, as in many things in life, first impressions are important, which is why I spend so much effort and care building up what barbecue pros call bark, known to the civilian world as crust. At its simplest, bark is the slightly salty, chewy, crispy result of cooking over direct heat or smoker-roasting. It involves the most miraculous transformation in all of cuisine, the Maillard reaction. Often mistakenly described as caramelizing—which is what happens when heat causes the natural sugars of carbohydrates to break down, resulting in vegetables that are golden brown and delicious—the Maillard reaction (named for a French chemist who led an adventuresome life in the late nineteenth and early twentieth centuries) describes what happens when a protein transforms under heat. It kicks off a chain reaction that is mind-numbingly complex, but all you need to remember is that it produces thousands of flavor compounds and these are what give browned meat its very distinct and appealing flavor.

Allowing the Maillard reaction to take place without burning the crust will give you robust flavor and chewy crispness. Rather than simply getting the fire to the right temperature and letting M. Maillard's discovery do its work, what I try to do in my cooking, throughout the process, is to create, deepen, accent, and enhance flavor. I look for every possible opportunity to deepen flavor, one step at a time, from seasoning to basting to aromatizing with wood smoke to mixing the juices from slicing the meat with the basting herbs I have used during the grilling.

BUILDING EXPLOSIVE FLAVOR

The ability to appreciate properly cooked meat is hardwired into our DNA. You don't need me to explain the difference between a blah crust and one that is irresistible. But in this chapter I tell you the indispensable, simple, often overlooked ways to create one.

THE FOUR SEASONS

Building flavor begins with seasoning. When it comes to seasoning before cooking, I often use just salt, black pepper, garlic salt, and cayenne. This is a big departure from the practice of most barbecue chefs (even myself at times), who create complex rubs with celery salt, onion powder, paprika, ground spices, and MSG, in addition to these four. In this, I take a page from the playbook of my good buddy, and pizza guru par excellence, Chris Bianco, who once told me, "The most important ingredient in cooking is restraint." This is tough in competition barbecue, where you get only one bite to impress the judges. Every trick in your book, every texture, every flavor has to be there in that first bite.

But that's not the way real people—even barbecue judges—eat in the real world. We take some meat, some sauce, and some vegetables, often on the same forkful. This approach calls for balance, not blowout, for the building and mixing of flavors and textures that seduce and ultimately satisfy—which gets me back to "the Four Seasons": salt, black pepper, garlic salt, and cayenne.

Why these four?

Salt is the most fundamental taste. Without it, meat is boring. In fact, almost everything is boring. It lifts all the other flavors, the way a rising tide lifts a boat.

Black pepper has warmth and a musky aroma. It helps to focus all the broad powerful flavors in barbecued food.

I've included garlic salt, which doesn't burn the way garlic powder does. It makes flavor punchier. It gives the Four Seasons focus, as well as a dimension of depth and aroma.

The spicy heat of cayenne wakes up all the other flavors in any food, and it adds the indefinable but pleasant quality of zing. A painter would say it puts down a base coat that is the foundation of a vibrant mahogany color. It's a signal from your eyes to your brain: "Here comes something delicious, so tell your mouth to start watering."

I apply the Four Seasons at the beginning of the process, before the meat touches the heat. They create a "meat paste" (see page 8), and when that hits the fire, it creates a wonderful base glaze that allows me to begin building flavor in the crust through basting.

I season again when I finish cooking, while the meat is still sizzling, using different highly flavored finishing salts (see page 240). This all came about following a discussion I had with one of my teachers when I was attending the Culinary Institute of America. One day, after his experimental kitchen class, the professor and I got to talking about the immense success of McDonald's french fries: unlike other fast-food fries, they're uniformly salty. Pondering how they achieved that consistency, we realized that the fries were salted at the instant they were taken from the fryer, when steam was still rising out of the interior of the fries and the fat was still dancing on the surface. So the salt dissolved in the moisture and evenly coated the fries.

The Four Seasons—salt, black pepper, garlic salt, and cayenne—contribute distinctive flavors and amplify all the other flavors in a recipe; at the same time, they are critical in helping to create a crust. That's the first part of any barbecued meat you taste when you take up knife and fork. A great crust is highly aromatic. It's like the overture to a symphony, or the barrage of artillery that precedes a battle: a powerful first encounter that leads into the full experience of the barbecued meat.

Truthfully, if you did no more than expose meat to the right kind of heat, you would get a crust, but the Four Seasons, applied at the right time and in the right way, will totally transform a crust.

FOUR SEASONS BLEND

Makes approximately 1 cup

1 cup sea or kosher salt
2 tablespoons freshly ground black pepper
2 tablespoons garlic salt
1 teaspoon cayenne pepper

• Combine the salt, black pepper, garlic salt, and cayenne in a small bowl.
Transfer to a spice grinder or clean coffee grinder and pulse to the
consistency of sand. Store in an airtight container for up to 1 month.

MAKING A MEAT PASTE: HOW TO SEASON

Season the meat all over with the Four Seasons Blend and/or other seasoning. Lightly moisten your hands and work the seasonings into the meat. Let the meat stand for 5 to 10 minutes. Through osmosis, the salt will penetrate the meat and push and pull out flavor components, creating what I call a "meat paste" on the surface. With more delicate flesh—fish, for example—you want to limit the amount of time that you allow this paste to form or you will risk "salt burn."

This paste—the combination of the seasonings and juices from the meat—will begin to form a glaze just as soon as you put the meat on the grill or in the smoker. Juices continue to escape from the meat and concentrate in the crust while a basting mixture adds more flavor. It's a win-win situation.

THE ART OF SCRUFFING

After seasoning the meat, I usually scruff it. Let me explain. One day, Jamie Oliver and I were preparing a meal on a ski trip with friends. We had just boiled up a big pot of potatoes. The French-trained part of my consciousness watched in horror as Jamie tossed the potatoes in a colander, shaking them vigorously.

"Brother," I said, hoping I could prevent my friend from committing a culinary crime. "What are you doing? You'll scar the potatoes!"

"I'm scruffing them up a bit," he said nonchalantly, explaining that by breaking up the smoothness of the potatoes, he was creating all kinds

---

HERB BASTING BRUSH

Rather than using an ordinary basting brush, I prefer to make my own by securing a bunch of herb sprigs (rosemary, sage, or thyme, or a combination, or other herbs, depending on what you are cooking) to a dowel, the handle of a wooden spoon, or a long-handled carving fork. The herb brush flavors the baste, releases oils into the crust as it builds, and eventually becomes a garnish for the Board Dressing (see page 27). Plus, it looks really cool and makes people think "Food!" when they see you using it.

It's important to season evenly, and on all sides. I call my technique "seasoning like rain." By seasoning from high up, you get more even distribution. Don't forget to season the sides, especially on thicker cuts.

You can hold pieces together, then roll and dab them on the board to pick up extra seasoning.

of nooks and crannies for a crust to develop: places where a baste or sauce could cling for extra flavor.

What's true for potatoes is equally true for meat. Eastern European grandmothers from time immemorial have known that the secret to a great pot roast is to really brown the meat, almost to the point of burning, and then rip it away from the pot when you turn it. The "roughed" meat has more surface area, because the tearing creates little indentations and each torn muscle fiber is one more place for the Maillard reaction to work its sorcery, creating hundreds of flavor compounds in the crust.

In grilling, meat gets scruffed when it sticks to the grate as you try to turn it over—especially on older grills. The slick, nonstick grates on newer grills, however, often don't tear the meat in this way. If you're using such a grill, or if you're cooking a smoother-muscled cut of meat, such as a boneless skinless chicken breast or a piece of rump, you should score it before you put it on the grill (see page 14), so there is more surface to grill and scruff up.

I'll grant you that you won't get those perfectly symmetrical crisscrossed lines of charring that you'll see on a fast-food burger or an Outback sirloin, but I will guarantee you that scruffing a cut of meat and building up layer upon layer of flavor is the way to max out flavor in any crust.

In the contest of beauty versus flavor and texture, remember: you don't taste beauty.

THE MEAT DANCE

Just as there is a right time to season, there's a right time to baste. Many barbecuers tend to baste before flipping. In my experience, this is exactly the wrong time: you end up soaking the crust, destroying the crispness you have worked so hard to develop, and burning a lot of the flavorful basting liquid, which hits the fire when you turn the meat. Basting after turning the meat instead of before makes all the difference in the world. The juices and fat on the side that has been exposed to the fire will be bubbling. You

Here is a pork chop properly scruffed and basted and tempered for an all-over even crusting.

SCRUFFING

When working with a nonstick grill, or to create more surface area in general, score the meat with a sharp knife in ¼- to ½-inch hash marks.

can hear the sound, like a tiny snare drum, as they fry the crust. Because those liquids pop and fizzle all over the surface of the meat, I call this the "dancing phase." This is the perfect time to apply your baste. There are many possibilities for bastes, but for my cooking, I have narrowed them down to a handful (see Bastes, page 226); usually they include some fat (rendered fat, trimmings from the meat itself, butter, or olive oil); garlic; a liquid—wine, vinegar, citrus juice, or stock; seasonings; and herbs.

When you baste the dancing, bubbling, or frying surface of cooked meat, a number of wonderful things happen. The fat in the baste crisps the crust just a little and then drips off the meat, so that you're creating aroma that adheres to the meat without adding significant fat calories. The acid (vinegar, wine, lemon juice) reduces into the crust, brightening the flavor. The heat from the meat releases the floral oils in the herbs, which combine in the crust to create subtle accents and a beautiful floral aroma.

Long story short, make sure that the meat is dancing before your baste gets into the act.

LAYERING FLAVOR

I had a moment of culinary clarity watching a Japanese grill chef in a Tokyo restaurant specializing in eel. Like so many of my fellow chefs, trained in the complicated and time-consuming craft of the sauces of French cuisine, I had become fascinated by the simple elegance of presentation, taste, and technique in Japanese cuisine.

The freshly caught eel was suspended over a bed of *binchotan* charcoal, which is made painstakingly from Japanese white oak and burns with a long, even, and intense heat. Rather than saturation-bombing the eel in a heavy sauce, the chef repeatedly flipped it and basted with a flavorful sauce that contained mirin, soy sauce, and sugar. (I learned that the sauce was always reinforced, never thrown out—interestingly, just as American grandmothers kept their buckwheat pancake starter going for months and months.) Instead of putting a concentrated sauce on in one fell swoop, he was building up layers of flavor. Each time the liquid came in contact with the hot flesh of the eel, it reduced and formed a thin glaze. After six or seven applications—flipping the eel each time—a clear amber glaze had formed. The end result was tender, moist, and delicate, enhanced immeasurably by the subtle but powerful glaze.

As you cook your way through the recipes in this book, you will see that I have taken the lesson of that unsung Japanese master to heart. Whenever I put something on the grill or in the smoker, I baste it repeatedly, accenting and building flavor every time.

I urge you to try my bastes on pages 226–39 instead of relying on just bottled sauce. Think of it as the difference between slapping a coat of rust-preventive paint on a piece of lawn furniture and building up the finish on an exquisite piece of lacquerware. Barbecue sauces may taste fine when you put a dab on your finger, but the taste is often lost or burned off in the cooking process. Achieving a flavorful crust requires constant layering, which is tough to do with a thick bottled sauce. This layering approach not only builds elegant and nuanced flavor, it momentarily cools the surface of the meat, which helps temper the meat (see Temper, Temper, page 20).

MAKING HEAT WORK FOR YOU

At its most basic level, cooking is nothing more than adding heat to ingredients, thereby transforming them. What many barbecuers forget is that you can control the heat rather than letting it control you.

Sometimes, this is as simple as being observant—for instance, notice how hot the side of your grill gets. If you're grilling a roast, you can use that heat to your advantage, positioning the meat so that it touches the one side of the grill.

A DIALOGUE WITH HEAT

In barbecuing meat, as in all things creative, you need to strike a fine balance. (A note about the word "meat": For simplicity's sake, I often use it to mean fish and poultry as well. "Meat" is a much more appetizing term than "protein," the generic used in cooking schools.) The goal is to cook the meat evenly and thoroughly, yet at the same time, you also don't want to overdo the crust, which takes so much loving care to bring to flavorful perfection. If you are grilling a thin cut of meat that you would like to serve rare or medium rare, the process is relatively quick. But large cuts like Rib Roast Done Like a Steak (page 71) or Smoked Pork Shoulder with Lime Coriander Salt (page 40) call for a lot more attention. Cooking a big piece of meat is like starting and then, more to the point, stopping a freight train. It takes a long time to get going and a long time to slow it down. After you remove a piece of meat from the fire, the internal temperature is going to keep going up. In chefspeak, this is known as "carryover cooking," and you need to keep it in mind as you cook.

The heart of all my barbecue techniques—I call it active grilling—is constantly monitoring the progress of heating the interior and building a crust. And even though I have turned out tens of thousands of cuts of meat in my restaurants, and rely on my sense of touch, feel, and experience, I still find that an instant-read thermometer is the best way to monitor the cooking process. You should use it to do the same. Whether you're cooking a thin cut of beef to serve medium rare or a long-cooked brisket, which you are serving well-done, you want to avoid toughness and keep the meat fibers moist and tender.

The difference between following directions, sitting back, and hoping for the best and, on the other hand, turning out spectacular tasting grilled food requires a constant dialogue with heat. Sometimes you will find the cooking is going a little too fast. This can result in a burnt or dried crust. There are many techniques throughout this book that you can use to adjust the heat to the ideal cooking temperature.

Cooking too quickly with too much heat can also push collagen-rich cuts (brisket, short ribs, pork shoulder, lamb breast—the classic tough cuts) past the critical window, which is an internal temperature between 160° and 170°F (71° and 77°C), when the collagen unravels and hydrates the meat fibers, making for a rich and unctuous mouthfeel. In order to maintain that plateau, the temperature in your cooking chamber— whether you are cooking in a highly calibrated, modern kitchen oven, a vertical smoker, a ceramic cooker, or your kettle barbecue—should be between 225° and 275°F (107° and 135°C). You need to monitor and control your heat.

Many beginning barbecuers freak when their pork shoulder reaches 165°F (74°C) and then plateaus there. They've all heard that you get the maximum falling-off the-bone tenderness at somewhere around 190°F

(88°C). So they raise the heat repeatedly. Still the thermometer doesn't budge. My advice? Don't freak: if you are cooking at the right temperature (usually between 225° and 275°F/107° and 135°C), let the meat do its thing—it will. If you turn up the heat, you will dry out the meat. And if you keep opening the door or raising the lid to check on the meat, you will lose moisture and heat momentum.

TEMPER, TEMPER

Cooking a piece of meat on the grill is a matter of building momentum so that heat travels evenly toward its center. Cooking meat properly is a question of controlling that momentum, maintaining just the right buildup of heat so that it transforms the meat in a uniform way. I call this art "tempering." Because it all takes place under the crust, out of sight, your only tools for gauging the process are experience, which will give you a sense of fire and doneness, and a thermometer.

The idea of tempering, which has become an obsession in my cooking, probably stems from an experience I had in 1996, when I was working at the Michelin-starred Château d'Isenbourg, in Alsace. We were asked to prepare a meal for the annual Group of 7 summit meeting, which was held in France that year. One of the sous chefs had lost track of the veal that we were preparing, and it took the quick reaction of the chef, an old pro named Didier—to come up with a way to save it. We—that is to say, all of us except for Chef Didier—thought the meat was ruined. But failure was not an option. The situation had to be rescued and it had to be done right away. Without saying anything, the chef pulled out a container of veal stock and

MAKING THE THERMOMETER FLOAT

Most people just stick the thermometer into the meat with one thrust and when they figure it's reached the middle, they take a reading. I find it's much more accurate if you insert it at an angle, particularly on thinner cuts. You get a much better feel for when it is in halfway. Then pull it in and out a few times: this is the "making it float" part. It creates a little slickness around the thermometer. The result is much more accurate than sticking it in and jamming it up against a few muscle fibers, hoping they are all done to exactly the same temperature.

immersed the endangered veal in the gelatinous cold stock. (It was like the chef version of *The Hurt Locker*, where one wrong move on the part of the Jeremy Renner character as he disarmed a bomb would have sent him to kingdom come.) His quick action arrested the buildup of heat, and when we finished off the veal in a hot roasting pan with some brown butter, the stock formed a beautiful glaze. The veal was nearly perfect, and you would never have known that the cooking process had gone off the rails at some point.

Ingenious, I thought. Chef Didier—from experience—had found a way to rescue meat that was on the verge of being overcooked. But while I had had my own share of rescue operations, the more important lesson was that only by constantly monitoring, observing, and reacting, as single-mindedly as possible, can one control how ingredients absorb heat and at what rate. Only by keeping to this path can you transform really good food into great food.

THE PAUSE BREAK

A lot of factors come into play in proper cooking: the heat of the fire, how far away the meat is from the coals, the temperature in the kitchen or outdoors, the temperature of the meat when you start. Remember, your goal is to bring the entire interior of the meat along at the same pace, so that it's evenly cooked, evenly colored, and a uniform temperature. Too much heat too soon can ruin the best cut of meat.

Letting the meat rest after cooking often results in juicy succulence, satisfying mouthfeel, and food that provides stick-to-your-ribs satisfaction. But I am of the firm belief that it is often important to rest meat *during* the cooking process, especially when dealing with thicker cuts.

I call this type of resting a "pause break." It allows the heat to be distributed more evenly: the outside crust slows down cooking while the center simultaneously gets ready for further cooking.

With cuts of meat that I want to serve rare, medium rare, or medium— for example, steak, lamb chops, and even pork chops—I'll often take the meat off the grill when the interior temperature reaches 100°F (38°C). And

THE MISSISSIPPI METHOD

Judging high, medium, and low heat is a subjective exercise. Holding your hand about 1 inch above the grill grate and counting "One Mississippi, two Mississippi, . . ." and so on until you have to pull your hand away is a time-honored way to do this. Everyone's hands are different and everyone has a different heat tolerance. I definitely have "chef's hands"—years in the kitchen and manning smokers and pits have seasoned my hands, so I am not as sensitive to heat as most people are. My recommendation is go with the rough guidelines below until you develop your own sense of low, medium, and high.

High	One Mississippi
Medium-high	One Mississippi, two
Medium	Count to three Mississippi
Medium-low	Count to four Mississippi
Low	Count to six Mississippi

I will allow it to rest for five to ten minutes so the heat, which has begun to penetrate and cook the meat, distributes evenly. Then I'll finish the steak by putting it back on the grill to further develop the crust and achieve a uniform juiciness and color. This pause break saves you from the commonplace overdone burnt crust, gray layer, raw center. The goal is to gently and gradually build up heat and then maintain it, so that it gets evenly distributed.

Look at resting as just another kind of heat control during cooking, like raising or lowering the flame or the grate. Knowing when to let meat rest and for how long is something that comes to you with experience, but all through the process an instant-read thermometer is indispensable. *I suggest an optimum temperature in every recipe in this book, but achieving it is always a gradual process,* so you want to use your instant-read thermometer to monitor the meat and thus to make sure it's cooking at the rate that will give you the best result.

Tip: When resting really big cuts of meat for longer than five minutes, I flip the meat at the midway point, because the top, which is exposed to the air, loses heat more rapidly than the bottom. Remember, gaining or losing heat uniformly is always the goal.

THE HOT POTATO METHOD

If asked to reduce my approach to grilling to just two words, they would be "hot potato." I treat meat on the grill as if I were handling a hot potato. When it gets really hot on one side (every couple of minutes) I flip it onto the other side. This is contrary to what many chefs do as they seek to create dark grill marks, but I couldn't care less about grill marks. I have been served plenty of food with nice grill marks that did nothing to disguise a poor cooking job and a lack of flavor and texture.

Notice I said "hot potato," not "warm potato." For the best results, I recommend a good strong wood fire (hardwood charcoal counts, or even briquettes—just not the kind impregnated with chemical fire starter). You can't beat real wood for pure, even, powerful heat. By constantly hot-potatoing—i.e., turning and moving—the meat, you can control the buildup of heat. And, if the crust is cooking too quickly, you can move the grilling surface farther from the fire (see the techniques described in High and Slow, page 58). Treat your fire as a tool that you control, rather than an act of nature that you can only react to. When you turn meat in this way, you are tempering it. The part that was closest to the coals and hottest is now exposed to the cooler air, which slows the cooking of the exterior while giving the interior a chance to catch up.

As soon as I turn the meat, I baste it, using an herb brush (see page 8). Basting also helps temper the meat. Then, as the fat in the basting mix gets hot, it crisps the surface while accentuating the flavor. The vinegar, stock, or other liquid in the baste adds another dimension and concentrates flavor as it reduces and evaporates. My goal throughout the tempering process is to treat the meat gently and gingerly.

By constantly turning the meat, and then basting the hot side right after, you build up flavor.

BOARD DRESSING

Once I have grilled a piece of meat, I want to capture the flavors of the delicious juices that emerge on the cutting board when I slice it and then build upon them, so I make what I call a board dressing. I often add some olive oil, or some of the rendered fat trimmings from the baste, or perhaps a little balsamic vinegar, to the juices.

For a basic Board Dressing, combine 6 tablespoons extra virgin olive oil, 2 tablespoons finely chopped fresh flat-leaf parsley, and sea or kosher salt and freshly ground black pepper to taste. You can improvise here, adding grated shallots or garlic (use a Microplane), finely chopped chiles, chopped scallions, and/or other chopped herbs, such as rosemary, thyme, and sage.

The secret flavorful last ingredient is the tip of the herb basting brush, chopped very fine and mixed into the dressing. After being in contact with the hot meat while it cooked, the rosemary, sage, or thyme will have softened a bit and released some aromatic and flavorful oils. I mix the herbs into the board dressing, then slice the meat, turning each slice in the dressing to coat. Then I pour the resulting board juices over the meat when I serve it.

So there you have it, the essence of what I have learned after years of grilling, more grilling, and then grilling some more. The thing that constantly amazes and satisfies me is that in this oldest form of cooking, I keep discovering new things to perfect my technique and increase my pleasure. May this book help you to do the same. I look forward to learning from your discoveries. Fire it up!

Part II

MEAT, FISH, AND FOWL

CLASSICS REVISITED

To begin the recipes in this book, I wanted to reconsider some old favorites in a new light, asking myself, "How can I simplify and tease out taste and texture so that they come together as elegantly and clearly as possible?"

This is a great lesson that I learned from one of my early mentors, Daniel Boulud. When he won four stars from *The New York Times* at Le Cirque, he did it in part by using the classic haute cuisine techniques that his masters had drummed into him in the greatest restaurants in France. But his secret weapon was that he had also looked to the stalwarts of family-style cooking and set himself the goal of "gastronomizing" the favorite dishes of his mother, and her mother, and all the French grandmothers for centuries before. Rather than cutting himself off from that tradition, he challenged himself to refine, focus, and deepen the flavors that he had learned to love as a boy. That is what I've attempted to do here. The classics are classics for a reason. People love them. They are great just the way they are, but my approach as a chef has always been: How do you take a good thing and make it better?

34 **Man Steak with
Thyme Zinfandel Salt**
The quintessential steak
with every texture known
to steakdom; super flavorful,
perfectly crusty.

40 **Smoked Pork Shoulder
with Lime Coriander Salt**
A brighter and lighter version
of an All-American classic;
really pumps up the
pork flavor.

42 **Roasted Rib Stack with
Worcestershire Salt**
Racks of ribs one on top of
the other, wrapped in bacon,
infused with a strong smoky,
salty, bacony flavor.

46 **Lamb in Ash Salt Crust
with Charcoal Salt**
Succulent shoulder with
the smoky perfume
of charcoal.

48 **Smoked Brisket on the Bone
with Chimichurri Crust**
The full monty of briskets—
all the fat, all the bones, all
the flavor.

50 **Double-Butterflied
Leg of Lamb**
An answer to a grill jockey's
prayer: a leg that cooks
uniformly on the grill.

54 **Smoked Crack-Back Chicken
with Lemon, Garlic, and
Herbes de Provence Baste**
The chicken's fat, flavor, and
juices, used as a baste and
glaze; crusty, crispy, and moist.

MAN STEAK
WITH THYME ZINFANDEL SALT

Serves 6 to 8

A very big steak. I'd seen it in Texas, but it wasn't until I got to England that I came across the name "man steak," no doubt because it is big, like an Englishman's appetite. It's somewhat haphazardly cut to include a few muscles in and around the rump, and it doesn't look like any recognizable steak. When you see a T-bone—or a rib eye or a shell steak—you know what it is right away. With the man steak, what I keep visualizing is an oversize hunk of meat on Fred Flintstone's grill.

This massive mix of muscles makes for a steak with varying textures and tenderness, which is interesting. I chose to start the book with this recipe because nothing says barbecue like a beautifully done steak. If you cook it right and baste it lovingly, let it rest, temper, and baste again, the result is an intensely flavorful crust and a juicy, toothsome interior.

One 6-pound "man steak" (see above)

¼ cup Four Seasons Blend (page 7)

1 tablespoon freshly ground black pepper

An herb brush (see page 8)

Basic Baste (page 230, made with the acid component)

Board Dressing (page 27)

Thyme Zinfandel Salt (page 250) for finishing

• Preheat the grill to medium-low.

• Season the beef all over with the seasoning blend and black pepper, then lightly moisten your hands with water and rub the seasonings into the meat. Allow to stand for 10 minutes to develop a "meat paste" (see page 8).

CONTINUED

It's big, it's juicy, it has every texture known to steakdom, something to satisfy every steak lover, with plenty more to choose from for the rest of the table. Steak doesn't get more dramatic or imposing.

• Put the beef on the clean (unoiled) grill grate and cook, without moving it, for 1 minute. Turn, grabbing the bone portion with your tongs, baste with the herb brush, and cook for 1 minute. Turn the steak, baste with the herb brush, and continue to cook, turning the meat every 2 minutes or so (see The Hot Potato Method, page 24) and basting each time you flip it, for 17 more minutes. The meat may stick and tear a bit, but this is OK, even desirable—the sticking and tearing is what I call "meat scruffing" (see page 8). The surface should begin to crust after scruffing. (For newer grills, where less sticking and tearing occurs, or for increased surface area, score with a knife—see page 14.) Transfer the steak to a large platter and allow to rest for 10 minutes.

• Meanwhile, clean and oil the grill grate.

• Put the steak back on the grill and cook, turning and basting it every 4 minutes, until the internal temperature registers 115°F on an instant-read thermometer for rare, 25 to 35 minutes.

• Meanwhile, pour the board dressing onto a cutting board (or mix it directly on the board). Finely chop the tip of the herb brush and mix the herbs into the dressing.

• Season the steak on both sides with the thyme salt, transfer to the cutting board, and allow to rest for 10 minutes.

• To serve, slice the meat ¼ inch thick, turning each slice in the dressing to coat, and arrange on plates. Pour the board juices over the meat and finish with a sprinkling of the thyme salt.

Turn, making sure to grab the bone portion with tongs (as I'm doing in the photo), and baste immediately with the herb brush.

CLEANING AS YOU COOK

The simple physics of barbecuing is
that carbonized food conducts heat
less evenly than clean metal. It is very
important that you clean the grill with
a wire brush before returning the meat
to the grill after its "pause break." That
way you will be putting the meat on an
evenly conductive surface. The steps
are brush; clean; turn; and baste.

SMOKED PORK SHOULDER WITH LIME CORIANDER SALT

Serves 8 to 12

For many Americans, especially those from the Deep South, "barbecue" is primarily a noun, often shortened to one syllable: "cue"—a term of affection that most often refers to pulled pork. While "cue" can mean the shredded meat of a whole hog, for most home barbecuers, and quite a few restaurants, it means the long-smoked meat of the pork shoulder. When it is prepared carefully, the shoulder goes through a remarkable transformation and the naturally tough meat becomes meltingly tender.

Pulled pork is a hearty dish, usually served on a bun with lots of strong sauce and maybe a dollop of coleslaw. My version is as unctuous as any you will find at a church supper or a Fourth of July picnic, but the flavors I add brighten and lighten the dish, accenting the savoriness of good pork. If you can find it, I strongly advise buying meat from a free-range animal, such as Niman Ranch pork, or the equivalent from your local farmers' market or other trusted source. It has real flavor that sauces and seasonings should enhance, not obscure.

One 7- to 8-pound bone-in pork butt

Basic Brine (page 238) or 8 cups Very Basic Brine (page 238)

¼ cup Four Seasons Blend (page 7)

Classic Southern Baste (page 234, made with the acid component)

An herb brush (see page 8)

Lime Coriander Salt (page 248) for finishing

• Put the pork in a large bowl or other container and add the brine. Cover and refrigerate for 24 hours.

• Preheat a smoker to 275°F.

• Remove the pork from the brine (discard the brine) and, while it is still moist, season it all over with the seasoning blend, working it in with your hands.

• Put the pork fat side up on the smoker grate and smoke for 2 hours. Transfer half the baste to a bowl and set aside for finishing.

• Baste the pork, using the herb brush, and continue to smoke, basting every hour, until the internal temperature registers 195°F on an instant-read thermometer, about 6 hours longer.

- Transfer the cooked shoulder to a bowl, cover tightly with plastic wrap, and allow to rest for 30 minutes.

- To serve, using two forks, pull the pork into chunks. Toss with the reserved baste and finish with a sprinkling of the lime coriander salt.

ROASTED RIB STACK
WITH WORCESTERSHIRE SALT

Serves 8 to 12

By stacking racks of ribs one on top of the other and wrapping them in bacon, I construct a thick "roast" out of three or four thinner cuts. The meat emerges more succulent than single racks of ribs would, infused with a strong smoky, salty, bacony flavor. The stack is smoked for 3 hours, then finished over direct heat.

4 racks St. Louis spareribs (about 2½ pounds each)

6 tablespoons Four Seasons Blend (page 7)

20 to 30 slices bacon

An herb brush (see page 8)

Classic Southern Baste (page 234; reserve the acid component to add later)

Board Dressing (page 27) or BBQ sauce, homemade or bottled (page 237)

Worcestershire Salt (page 252) for finishing

• Season the ribs all over with the seasoning blend. Stack the racks on top of each other, laying a strip of bacon between each layer. Starting at one end, drape a slice of bacon over the entire stack, allowing it to hang down evenly on both sides. Place another slice of bacon next to the first one, overlapping it by ¼ inch. Continue down the entire length of the stack, covering it from end to end. Wrap tightly in plastic wrap and then in heavy-duty aluminum foil and refrigerate for 30 minutes.

• Preheat a smoker to 275°F.

• Put the wrapped stack round side up on the smoker grate and smoke for 1 hour.

• Remove the ribs from the smoker and unwrap. Place back on the smoker, continue to cook for 2 hours, and then remove.

• Preheat a grill to medium.

• Remove the bacon from the outside of the rack. Finely chop and set aside to add to the board dressing or sauce. Separate the slabs of ribs (reserving the bacon between the layers as well) and lightly coat with the fat portion of baste. Add the acid component to the baste.

- Put the racks top side down on the clean (unoiled) grill grate and grill, turning and basting them every 5 minutes or so, until crisp and browned on both sides, about 45 minutes. The meat should be tender but not falling apart.

- Meanwhile, pour the board dressing or BBQ sauce onto a cutting board (or mix the dressing directly on the board). If using the dressing, finely chop the tip of the herb brush and mix the herbs into the dressing. Mix the chopped bacon into the dressing or BBQ sauce, if desired.

- Season the ribs on both sides with the Worcestershire salt and transfer to the cutting board. Cut into individual ribs, turning each rib to coat in the dressing or sauce, and transfer to plates or a platter. Finish with a sprinkling of the Worcestershire salt and serve.

Wrapping a stack of ribs in bacon seals in juiciness, adds smoky seasoning, and promotes even roasting. As the ribs cook inside their "bacon envelope," they develop extra-juicy succulence.

LAMB IN ASH SALT CRUST WITH CHARCOAL SALT

Serves 6 to 8

Because lamb is a young animal, its meat has a higher percentage of collagen in relation to muscle than that from a more mature animal. This is a gift to the chef, because it means that when the lamb is cooked long and slow, the collagen turns to gelatin and the meat gets more and more succulent until it reaches that nirvanic state that I think of as "melty." Encasing the lamb shoulder and breasts in a crust of ash and salt perfumes the meat with the smokiness of charcoal, and then, as the salt case solidifies, flavorful steam is driven into the meat—almost like a gentle pressure cooker. Charcoal salt seasoning at the end reinforces the smoky, salty flavor.

2 boneless lamb breasts (about 1 pound each), cut crosswise in half

One 4-pound bone-in lamb shoulder

⅓ cup Four Seasons Blend (page 7)

½ cup fresh thyme leaves

½ cup fresh rosemary leaves

6 pounds coarse sea or kosher salt

4 cups ashes (from a previous fire)

10 large egg whites

1 cup Lemon Oregano Baste (page 231, made with the acid component)

Charcoal Salt (page 253) for finishing

• Preheat a smoker to 275°F.

• Season the lamb breasts and shoulder on all sides with the seasoning blend, rubbing it into the meat. Set aside.

• Mix the thyme and rosemary together.

• Combine the salt, ashes, and egg whites in a large bowl, mixing well. Spread a 1-inch-thick layer of the salt mixture in the bottom of a baking pan that will hold the lamb comfortably, and set on a baking sheet. Arrange 2 pieces of the lamb breast fat side down on top of the salt. Scatter ½ cup of the herbs on top of the breast pieces, then arrange the shoulder on top. Scatter the remaining ½ cup herbs over the shoulder, and cover with the remaining 2 breast pieces. Cover the lamb with the remaining salt mixture, patting it onto the meat so it is completely covered.

- Put the lamb in the smoker and cook for 5 hours. Remove from the smoker and allow to rest for 15 to 20 minutes.

- Crack the salt crust all around the sides and pull off the top of the crust. Transfer the lamb to a large serving platter and, using two forks, shred the meat, pulling the shoulder meat away from the bone. Toss with the baste and finish with a sprinkling of the charcoal salt. Or, if you like, take the whole dish to the table, crack the crust and remove the top, and let your guests pick at the meat and season it with the baste and salt to taste.

Grating a tiny amount of charcoal into your finishing salt gives you that extra smoky burnt-wood accent. But don't use a resinous wood like pine and *never* cook with chemically treated wood.

SMOKED BRISKET ON THE BONE
WITH CHIMICHURRI CRUST

Serves 10 to 12

A bone-in rib roast is a familiar but dramatic and impressive presentation at a family gathering. So why not a bone-in brisket? Instead of the temperamental thin point, the boneless cut that most markets sell, this is the full monty of brisket. It has every muscle; every piece of fat cap, to melt and bathe the meat; and all the bones, which conduct heat and juicy steam into the interior. I first learned to love brisket at my grandmother's table. Then I studied with the pitmasters of the American heartland to learn the long-smoking technique. The pièce de résistance here is my version of tart, garlicky, herbal chimichurri sauce, a staple among Argentine gauchos.

It may take some doing to find a whole bone-in brisket, but if your butcher or the manager of the meat section in the supermarket has any sense of adventure at all, give it a try. And ask him to save the fat trim from the brisket—or from another cut—to use for basting the meat.

One 14-pound bone-in brisket

½ cup Four Seasons Blend (page 7)

2 pounds beef fat, cut into 20 long ½-inch-thick strips

6 cups Chimichurri Baste (page 233, made with the acid component)

An herb brush (see page 8)

Board Dressing (page 27)

Wine Vinegar Salt (page 251) for finishing

• Preheat the smoker to 275°F.

• Season the brisket all over with the seasoning blend, then lightly moisten your hands with water and work the seasonings into the meat. Allow to stand for 10 minutes to develop a "meat paste" (see page 8).

• Put the brisket bone side down on the smoker grate. Arrange the strips of fat on a rack above the brisket to render and baste the meat as it cooks (if you don't have a rack, arrange the strips on the brisket). Smoke for 3 hours.

• Remove the brisket from the smoker and put it bone side down in a roasting pan. Spread about 2 cups of the chimichurri over the meat and add 2 cups water to the pan.

• Smoke the brisket for 4 hours longer, using the herb brush to baste it every hour; give it a final baste 10 to 15 minutes before it is done. Remove the brisket from the smoker, baste with the pan drippings, and allow to rest for 20 minutes.

• Meanwhile, pour the board dressing onto a cutting board (or mix it directly on the board). Finely chop the tip of the herb brush and mix the herbs into the dressing.

• To serve, carve the brisket against the grain into ¼-inch-thick slices, turning each slice in the dressing to coat, and finish with a sprinkling of the wine vinegar salt.

Macerating and smearing the herbs into the oil is a key step in making your board dressing.

DOUBLE-BUTTERFLIED LEG OF LAMB

Serves 6 to 8

In the last fifteen or twenty years, barbecued boneless leg of lamb has become a grilling favorite. The usual scenario is something like this: The thin part of the butterflied leg is done in thirty minutes or so. But then there is the thick part. It never seems to get done. You probe it for temperature. Not believing that any piece of meat could take that long, you start to cut into it . . . repeatedly, so that the juices flow out. By the time it is cooked through, it is as dry as a parched cornfield after a year-long drought, and the thin part is completely overdone.

My solution is to butterfly the whole boneless leg and then butterfly the thicker part again so that the lamb is all uniformly thick at approximately 1½ inches. And I start by cooking it fat side down, weighted with a brick or two placed on top of a piece of wood that sits on the lamb to keep it flat so the whole cut is exposed to the heat of the grill grate.

One 4-pound boneless leg of lamb, "double-butterflied" (see above)

3 tablespoons Four Seasons Blend (page 7)

2 tablespoons freshly ground black pepper

An herb brush (see page 8)

Lemon Oregano Baste (page 231; reserve the vinegar to add later)

Board Dressing (page 27)

Thyme, Rosemary, and Sage Salt (page 244) for finishing

• Preheat the grill to medium-low.

• Season the lamb all over with the seasoning blend and black pepper, then lightly moisten your hands with water and work the seasonings into the meat. Allow to stand for 10 minutes to develop a "meat paste" (see page 8).

• Using the herb brush, coat the lamb lightly with some of the fat portion of the baste. Add the reserved vinegar to the remaining baste and set aside.

• Put the lamb fat side down on the well-oiled clean grill grate and cover with a lid. Cook, without moving the meat, for 12 minutes. Turn and baste the meat. Cook for 6 minutes longer—if there's flare-up re-cover with the lid. Transfer to a large platter and allow to rest for 5 minutes.

• Meanwhile, clean the grill grate.

- Put the lamb back on the grill and cook, turning and basting once, until the internal temperature registers 130°F on an instant-read thermometer, about 8 minutes.

- Meanwhile, pour the board dressing onto a cutting board (or mix it directly on the board). Finely chop the tip of the herb brush and mix the herbs into the dressing.

- Transfer the lamb to the cutting board, cut into pieces about 2 inches by 2 inches, turning them in the dressing to coat, and transfer to plates or a platter. Finish with a sprinkling of the herb salt and serve.

By double-butterflying a leg of lamb
to a uniform thickness, it becomes
possible to grill the whole thing evenly
all at once, a pretty neat trick.

SMOKED CRACK-BACK CHICKEN WITH LEMON, GARLIC, AND HERBES DE PROVENCE BASTE

Serves 4

Ask any French chef worth his toque what his favorite meal is, and the answer will be a perfect roast chicken served with a laboriously prepared sauce. The secret is roasting the bones and caramelizing the juices that are then extracted in the lengthy stock-making process. Take my word for it, I haven't met many home cooks who go to such lengths. In fact, most restaurant chefs don't either, leaving that task to the lower ranks of their kitchen brigade.

My solution is to crack the bones of the intact chicken, then stab it repeatedly. The result looks like a chicken that ran into a truck. But by cracking the bones and stabbing, I can smoke the chicken whole and still get the flavor-rich juices from the bones.

I put the bird in a cast-iron pan in a smoker, so that instead of losing the fat, flavor, and juices to the coals, they collect in the bottom of the pan. Then I use them to baste and glaze the chicken to produce a crust as deeply flavored and crispy as any Parisian pullet. The brine adds flavor, of course, but it also preserves moisture, which is critical to keep the white meat from drying out while the longer-cooking dark meat finishes.

One 3½-pound chicken

Basic Brine (page 238) or 8 cups Very Basic Brine (page 238)

1 tablespoon Four Seasons Blend (page 7)

An herb brush (see page 8)

1 cup Lemon, Garlic, and Herbes de Provence Baste (page 232; reserve the acid component to add later)

VEGETABLES

½ cup finely chopped shallots

¼ cup finely chopped carrots

¼ cup finely chopped celery

6 bay leaves, preferably fresh

1 tablespoon fresh thyme leaves

½ cup dry white wine

1½ cups chicken stock or canned low-sodium broth

2 tablespoons cold unsalted butter, cut into small cubes

2 tablespoons finely chopped fresh flat-leaf parsley

Lemon Thyme Salt (page 246) for finishing

- Crack the back of the chicken by placing it on its side and pressing down on it (see first photo, next page). Then, holding the breast, tap and lightly smash the back of the chicken until it feels like a tight bag of marbles. Insert a thin sharp knife into the back of the chicken to make about 10 evenly spaced holes, pushing the knife through the carcass and twisting it.

- Put the chicken in a large heavy-duty plastic bag or a bowl and add the brine. Seal the bag or cover the bowl and refrigerate for 24 hours.

- Put a large cast-iron skillet in a smoker and preheat the smoker to 350°F.

- Remove the chicken from the brine (discard the brine) and, while it is still moist, season it all over with the seasoning blend, working it in with your hands. Truss the chicken.

- Using the herb brush, moisten the chicken on all sides with some of the fat portion of the baste. Add the acid component to the remaining baste and set aside.

- Put the chicken breast side up in the preheated skillet and smoke for 10 minutes. Turn it on its side, baste lightly, and cook for 10 minutes. Turn it onto the other side, baste lightly, and cook for another 10 minutes.

- Turn the chicken breast side up and scatter the vegetables and herbs around it. Cook for 20 minutes.

- Add the white wine to the pan and cook for 10 minutes, or until the internal temperature of the thigh registers 160°F on an instant-read thermometer. Transfer the chicken to a platter (set the pan aside) and allow to rest for 10 to 15 minutes.

- Meanwhile, boil the pan juices over medium heat until reduced to a glaze. Add the chicken stock and boil until reduced by half. Swirl in the butter piece by piece, then pass the sauce through a fine strainer into a sauceboat or small serving bowl. Stir in the chopped parsley.

- Serve the chicken, whole or cut up, sprinkled with the lemon thyme salt. Pass the sauce at the table.

"Crack" the chicken by placing it on its side and pressing down to crack the back. Take a rolling pin or the back of a wine bottle and, while holding the breast, begin to tap and smash the back. Continue several times until the back feels like a tight bag of marbles. Then insert a knife into the back area, making 10 evenly spaced holes, putting the knife completely through and twisting.

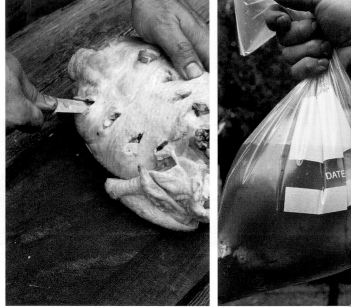

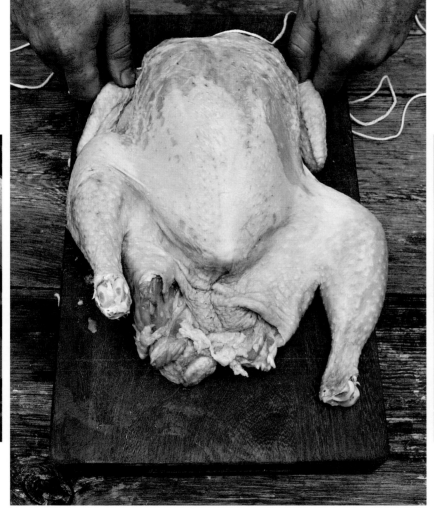

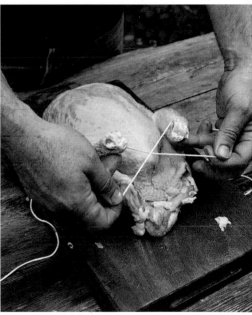

Remove the chicken from the brine and, while it is still moist, apply the seasoning mix, working it in with your hands. Discard any used brine. Then truss the chicken.

HIGH AND SLOW

"Low and slow" is an article of barbecue faith, repeated so many times that I doubt that people ever give it a second thought.

Well, I have, and I disagree. It's not that cooking for a long time over low heat can't produce great food. It has, it does, and it will continue to do so. But that isn't the whole story. In this and the following chapter, I explore two other approaches: high and mostly slow, and low and fast.

The high-and-mostly-slow method is particularly good for larger cuts. What got me thinking in this direction was the pit barbecue method, which became popular in the South long before the invention of rotisserie smokers and charcoal briquettes.

In those simpler times, you dug a hole, or stacked some bricks to make a fireplace, filled it with logs, and lit the fire. When the fire was at the perfect temperature, you put a grate over the pit and started to cook. If you wanted less heat, you let the fire burn down, raked the fire, or raised the grate. The lower temperatures achieved by cooking at a distance allows the crust to develop slowly and the heat to penetrate the interior of the meat more gradually and uniformly. These are good things.

The advantage pit cooking has over cooking closer to a less powerful fire is that you don't lose the flavor-building atomization that you get when meat, high off the grill, drips onto a strong fire. The juices, fat, and basting liquids hit the fire and are superheated to form a smoke-flavored, aroma-rich steam that bathes the meat all through the long, slow cooking process. My "elevated grate" produces the same result as a pit, but you don't need to spend a day digging a hole big enough to accommodate a casket.

A lot of the secret of successful barbecue is using your judgment and adapting to conditions. What kind of wood are you using? How hot does it burn? How long? Is there wind that blows some of the heat and flavorful smoke away (and also tempers the meat)?

My wrinkle on the high-and-slow technique is the fast finish part of the equation that kicks in when I lower the grate and finish the cooking closer to the fire, basting rapidly and often. This sets up the finish on the bark, or crust, to best effect. Result: perfect crust, juicy meat, and pervasive flavorful smoke.

ELEVATING THE GRATE

You can buy a grill with a hand-cranked wheel that allows you to raise and lower the cooking surface. Or you can save yourself a lot of money and buy an extra grate for your grill, using bricks to elevate it above the main grill grate.

62   **High-Low Boneless Rib Eye**
Super flavor, super crusty,
tender through and through.

66   **High-Low Center-
Cut Tenderloin
(aka Chateaubriand)**
The most popular cut in
my restaurant; incredibly
tender yet superbly crusty.

68   **Filet Mignon**
My favorite way to make
filet: smoky and tender.

71   **Rib Roast Done Like a Steak**
Aka the World's Thickest
Steak—extra crust,
juicier meat.

76   **Thick Pork Chops,
Guaranteed Juicy**
A solution to dry pork chops:
make 'em thicker, cook 'em
slower, baste 'em often.

80   **Leg of Lamb**
Perfectly herbaceous,
crispy, lamby crust.

HIGH-LOW BONELESS RIB EYE

Serves 4

A rib eye is, in many ways, the most satisfying steak. Its gnarly marbled surface makes it very scruffable (see The Art of Scruffing, page 8) so that it develops a great crust that accepts basting well. The eye of the roast is superflavorful and, like a tenderloin, is best served in the medium-rare-to-rare stage. The deckle, or outside strip, about an inch or two thick, is so marbled that it should be a bit more well-done, at which point it has both deep flavor and the hard-to-achieve tenderness of a perfect brisket. Although the classic French way to do a rib eye is on the bone (*côte de boeuf;* aka cowboy cut in the USA), I prefer boneless for this high-low style. It makes it easier to develop a crust on all sides of the meat. To achieve a more well-done deckle, and to crisp the exterior and render more fat, I prop the steak up for a few minutes on each edge so that only the deckle is exposed to the heat source.

Four 14- to 16-ounce boneless rib eye steaks, at least 2½ inches thick

3 tablespoons Four Seasons Blend (page 7)

1 tablespoon coarsely ground black pepper

An herb brush (see page 8)

2 cups baste of your choice (pages 230–34, made with the acid component)

Board Dressing (page 27)

A clean brick, wrapped in foil

• Set up the grill with an elevated grate (see page 59) and preheat it to high.

• Season the steaks on both sides with the seasoning blend and pepper, then lightly moisten your hands with water and work the seasonings into the meat. Allow to stand for 10 minutes to develop a "meat paste" (see page 8).

• Put the steaks on the clean (unoiled) grill grate and cook, without moving them, for 1 minute. Turn, making sure to grab the "eye" portion of each steak with your tongs (see third photo, page 64), and cook for 1 minute. The meat may stick and tear a bit, but this is OK, even desirable—the sticking and tearing is what I call "meat scruffing" (see page 8). (For newer grills, where less sticking and tearing occurs, or for increased surface area, score with a knife—see page 14.) Put the foil-wrapped brick on the grill grate to be used as a steady point for the beef, lean the steaks up against it, and cook for 2 minutes, then turn the steaks and repeat until you've cooked them for 2 minutes each on all four edges.

- Move the brick to the side and continue cooking the steaks, turning them every 1 to 2 minutes (see The Hot Potato Method, page 24) and basting with the herb brush each time you flip them, until the internal temperature registers 95°F on an instant-read thermometer, about 12 minutes longer.

- Transfer the steaks to a platter, brush lightly with the baste, and let rest for at least 5 minutes, and up to 30 minutes.

- Meanwhile, carefully remove the elevated grill grate.

- Put the steaks on the hot grill and cook, turning every 1 to 2 minutes and basting lightly every time the beef is moved, until the internal temperature registers 115°F, about 10 minutes.

- Meanwhile, pour the board dressing onto a cutting board (or mix it directly on the board). Finely chop the tip of the herb brush and mix the herbs into the dressing.

- Transfer the steaks to the cutting board and turn them in the dressing to coat. Allow to rest for 5 to 10 minutes.

- To serve, slice the meat ¼ inch thick, turning each slice in the dressing to coat, and arrange on plates, then pour some of the board juices over each serving.

Turn, making sure to grab the "eye"
portion, not the deckle, with tongs.

Continue to cook an additional
2 minutes on each of the four edges.

HIGH-LOW CENTER-CUT TENDERLOIN (AKA CHATEAUBRIAND)

Serves 8 to 10

This is the most popular cut in my restaurants. I think of chateaubriand as "the sociable cut."

"Why?" you might ask. Because it is so tender that it doesn't stop conversation. When you have a table full of people chomping away on a marbled rib eye or brisket, there is much more time spent navigating the cut than chatting.

As an active griller I appreciate the way you can turn and roll the meat so easily, the way hot dogs roll around on those metal rods in the movie theater. And by using tongs, you can "drive" the meat to hotter and cooler areas of the cooking surface. This puts the chef more in control.

Three 1¼-pound center-cut beef tenderloin roasts, trimmed and tied every 2 inches with kitchen string

¼ cup Four Seasons Blend (page 7)

An herb brush (see page 8)

2 cups baste of your choice (pages 230–34, made with the acid component)

Board Dressing (page 27)

- Set up the grill with an elevated grate (see page 59) and preheat it to high.

- Season the beef all over with the seasoning blend, then lightly moisten your hands with water and work the seasonings into the meat. Allow to stand for 5 minutes to develop a "meat paste" (see page 8).

- Put the beef on the clean (unoiled) grill grate and cook, without moving it, for 2 minutes. Roll each roast a quarter turn and cook for 2 minutes, then turn each roast again and repeat until you've cooked them for 2 minutes each on all four sides. The meat may stick and tear a bit, but this is OK, even desirable—the sticking and tearing is what I call "meat scruffing" (see page 8). (For newer grills, where less sticking and tearing occurs, or for increased surface area, score with a knife—see page 14.)

- Give the roasts a quarter turn, baste with the herb brush, and continue cooking, rolling each roast a quarter turn every 2 minutes or so (see The Hot Potato Method, page 24) and basting each time the meat is moved, until the internal temperature registers 95°F on an instant-read thermometer, 7 to 12 minutes longer.

- Transfer the roasts to a platter, brush lightly with the baste, and let rest for at least 5 minutes, and up to 30 minutes.

- Meanwhile, carefully remove the elevated grill grate.

- Put the beef on the hot grill and cook, turning the roasts every minute or two and basting lightly every time the meat is moved, until the internal temperature registers 110°F, 5 to 10 minutes.

- Meanwhile, pour the board dressing onto a cutting board (or mix it directly on the board). Finely chop the tip of the herb brush and mix the herbs into the dressing.

- Transfer the roasts to the cutting board and roll in the dressing to coat. Allow to rest for 5 to 10 minutes.

- To serve, slice the beef ¼ inch thick, turning each slice in the dressing to coat, and arrange on plates. Pour some of the board juices over each serving.

The simplest way to barbecue with the high-low method is to put a second grate on top of two stacks of bricks. This increases your distance from a hot fire and gives you uniform radiant heat.

FILET MIGNON

Serves 8 to 10

Filet mignon is popular chiefly because it is so tender. That's why it is important to develop a flavorful crust for contrast. The high-low method is particularly well suited to the task. You can cook at low to moderate heat by putting the steaks at a good distance from a strong fire. The strength of the fire accounts for heavy aromatizing of the fat and juices as they hit the flames and rise up as a smoky perfume that infuses the meat. Then, at the end of the process, you close the deal with the crust, firming and finishing with quick, frequent "hot potato" turning nearer to the fire. This is my favorite way to cook filet mignon.

Eight to ten 8-ounce filets mignons, about 2 inches thick

3 tablespoons Four Seasons Blend (page 7)

An herb brush (see page 8)

2 cups baste of your choice (pages 230–34, made with the acid component)

Board Dressing (page 27)

- Set up the grill with an elevated grate (see page 59) and preheat it to high.

- Season the filets mignons on both sides with the seasoning blend, then lightly moisten your hands with water and work the seasonings into the meat. Allow to stand for 5 minutes to develop a "meat paste" (see page 8).

- Put the beef on the clean (unoiled) grill grate and cook, without moving the steaks, for 2 minutes. Turn and cook for 2 minutes on the other side. The meat may stick and tear a bit, but this is OK, even desirable—the sticking and tearing is what I call "meat scruffing" (see page 8). (For newer grills, where less sticking and tearing occurs, or for increased surface area, score with a knife—see page 14.) Then turn the steaks on their sides and grill for about 1 minute each on all four edges.

- Continue cooking, turning the steaks over every minute or so (see The Hot Potato Method, page 24) and basting with the herb brush each time the meat is moved, until the internal temperature registers 95°F on a instant-read thermometer, 5 to 9 minutes longer.

- Transfer the steaks to a platter, brush lightly with the baste, and let rest for at least 5 minutes, and up to 30 minutes.

- Meanwhile, carefully remove the elevated grill grate.

- Put the steaks on the hot grill and cook, turning every 1 to 2 minutes and basting lightly every time the beef is moved, until the internal temperature registers 110°F, about 5 minutes.

- Meanwhile, pour the board dressing onto a cutting board (or mix it directly on the board). Finely chop the tip of the herb brush and mix the herbs into the dressing.

- Transfer the steaks to the cutting board and turn them in the dressing to coat. Allow to rest for 5 minutes, no longer.

- To serve, transfer the steaks to plates and pour the board juices over them.

RIB ROAST DONE LIKE A STEAK

Serves 8 to 10

If there were ever a recipe that represented the whole Adam Perry Lang Playbook, this is it: active and aggressive with scruffing, mucho basting, tempering, the Maillard reaction, board dressing. I split the bones apart a bit to create more surface area for the heat to penetrate. Then I pound the meat. It has a similar effect to pounding a veal cutlet or a chicken breast, except in this case my goal is not to flatten a rib roast to a 2½-inch scaloppine. My intention in pounding is to compress the meat, adding density and creating more surface area for the crust to develop and incorporate flavor. When I demonstrated this technique to the guys in my butcher shop, they thought I was crazy—that is, until they shared one with me.

Note: This recipe is an example par excellence of the use of board dressing. So much time is spent seasoning and flavoring the crust that if you didn't add board dressing at the end to balance the flavor, even the best aged prime meat wouldn't be shown to its full advantage.

Two 4¼- to 4½-pound 2- to 3-bone rib roasts, "prepped like a steak"

6 tablespoons Four Seasons Blend (page 7)

2 tablespoons coarsely ground black pepper

An herb brush (see page 8)

4 cups baste of your choice (pages 230–34, made with the acid component)

Board Dressing (page 27)

A clean brick, wrapped in foil

- Set up the grill with an elevated grate (see page 59) and preheat it to high.

- Season the beef all over with the seasoning blend and pepper, then lightly moisten your hands with water and work the seasonings into the meat. Allow to stand for 10 minutes to develop a "meat paste" (see page 8).

CONTINUED

- Put the beef on the clean (unoiled) grill grate and cook, without moving it, for 1 minute. Turn, making sure to grab the "eye" portion of each steak with your tongs (see third photo, page 64), and cook for 1 minute. The meat may stick and tear a bit, but this is OK, even desirable—the sticking and tearing is what I call "meat scruffing" (see page 8). (For newer grills, where less sticking and tearing occurs, or for increased surface area, score with a knife—see page 14.) Turn the meat and cook for 3 minutes, then flip and cook for 3 minutes longer.

- Put the foil-wrapped brick on the grill grate to be used as a steady point for the beef, lean the meat up against it, and cook for 4 minutes. Turn the roasts and repeat until you've cooked them for 4 minutes each on all four edges.

- Move the brick to the side and continue cooking the roasts, turning them every 3 to 4 minutes (see The Hot Potato Method, page 24) and basting with the herb brush each time the meat is moved, until the internal temperature registers 105°F on an instant-read thermometer, 25 to 30 minutes.

- Transfer the beef to a platter, brush lightly with the baste, and let rest for at least 5 minutes, and up to 30 minutes.

- Remove the brick from the grate and carefully remove the elevated grill grate.

- Put the roasts on the hot grill and cook, turning every 3 to 4 minutes and basting lightly every time the beef is moved, until the internal temperature registers 120°F.

- Meanwhile, pour the board dressing onto a cutting board (or mix it directly on the board). Finely chop the tip of the herb brush and mix the herbs into the dressing.

- Transfer the roasts to the cutting board and turn them in the dressing to coat. Allow to rest for 5 to 10 minutes.

- To serve, cut the meat off the bones, cut the bones apart, and put the bones back on the grill. Slice the meat ¼ inch thick, turning each slice in the dressing to coat, and arrange on plates. Pour some of the board juices over each serving, and serve with the bones on a platter alongside.

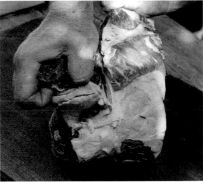

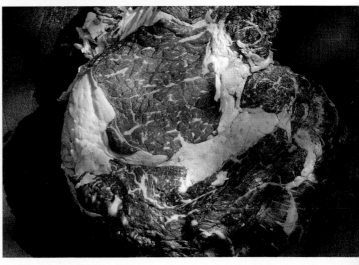

This is the steakiest steak in the book:
a beautiful, well-seasoned rib roast,
cooked high-low, and tempered along
the way, then finished with a board
dressing of meat juice and herbs. Once
you've perfected this recipe, you are a
true master of charred and scruffed.

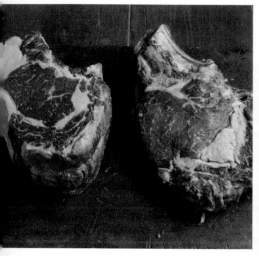

THICK PORK CHOPS, GUARANTEED JUICY

Serves 8 to 10

If you have a problem cooking pork chops so that they are juicy and succulent, rather than dry and tough, you are not alone. The eye of the loin of a pig, where all pork chops come from, is not a very well marbled piece of meat. For that matter, neither is a beef filet mignon or a lamb chop. If you cook any of them past medium-rare, or at most rosy pink, they lose all succulence and flavor.

By brining these extra-thick bone-in pork chops and tempering them with flavor bastes and frequent turning, à la hot potato style, the heat transfer is uniform, the crust development is highly flavorful, and the meat turns out mouthwateringly juicy. The high-low style is the very best way that I have found to serve the stern masters of crustiness and juiciness.

Tip: Remember there are more than two sides to these substantial chops of pig. In addition to applying radiant and direct heat to the top and bottom, you need to do the same for all the other facets of the chops, including the bone side. To do this, I prop the chops against a brick and cook briefly on all four edges. The aim is to expose all surfaces to the heat in order to create a crust and transfer heat from all directions.

Eight to ten 16- to 18-ounce double pork rib chops, at least 2½ inches thick

Basic Brine (page 238) or 8 cups Very Basic Brine (page 238)

3 tablespoons Four Seasons Blend (page 7)

An herb brush (see page 8)

1 cup Habanero Syrup (page 237)

Board Dressing (page 27)

A clean brick, wrapped in foil

- Put the pork chops in a large heavy-duty plastic bag or large bowl and add the brine. Seal the bag or cover the bowl and refrigerate for at least 12 hours, and up to 16 hours.

- Set up the grill with an elevated grate (see page 59) and preheat it to high.

- Remove the chops from the brine (discard the brine) and pat dry lightly with paper towels. Season the chops on both sides with the seasoning blend, then lightly moisten your hands with water and work the seasonings into the meat. Allow to stand for 10 minutes to develop a "meat paste" (see page 8).

• Put the pork chops on the clean (unoiled) grill grate and cook, without moving them, for 1 minute, then turn and cook for 1 minute on the other side. Turn and cook for 2 minutes, then flip and cook for 2 minutes longer; repeat two more times. The meat may stick and tear a bit, but this is OK, even desirable—the sticking and tearing is what I call "meat scruffing" (see page 8). (For newer grills, where less sticking and tearing occurs, or for increased surface area, score with a knife—see page 14.)

CONTINUED

- Put the foil-wrapped brick on the grill grate to be used as a steady point for the pork chops, lean the chops up against it, and cook for 1 minute. Turn the chops and repeat until you've cooked them for 1 minute each on all four edges.

- Move the brick to the side and continue cooking, turning the chops every minute or so (see The Hot Potato Method, page 24) and, using the herb brush, basting with the habanero syrup each time the meat is moved, until the internal temperature registers 115°F on an instant-read thermometer.

- Transfer the pork chops to a platter, brush lightly with the syrup, and let rest for at least 10 minutes, and up to 30 minutes.

- Meanwhile, carefully remove the elevated grill grate.

- Put the chops on the grill and cook, turning often and basting lightly every time the pork is moved, until the internal temperature registers 130° to 135°F.

- Meanwhile, pour the board dressing onto a cutting board (or mix it directly on the board). Finely chop the tip of the herb brush and mix the herbs into the dressing.

- Transfer the chops to the cutting board and turn them in the dressing to coat. Allow to rest for 5 to 10 minutes.

- To serve, arrange the chops on plates and pour the board juices over them.

When juices and fat drip down fro
the meat onto the coals, they atom
and infuse the meat with flavor.

LEG OF LAMB

Serves 6 to 8

Lamb, especially leg of lamb, is one of the more forgiving meats—unless you make a conscious effort and really take it too far, it is pretty hard to ruin it. This is not an argument for careless cooking, it's just my way of saying that I can eat it rare, medium, or well-done—which is exactly what you get when you cook a leg. The leg tapers from thick to thin, so you will get all levels of doneness. One of its great virtues is that the collagen-rich parts—which tend to be the areas that get well-done—become very unctuous. The result is mouthwatering and very satisfying. It has a lot to do with the fact that lamb is a young animal. Its fat is new and fresh, not mature. The same can be said of veal, which is one of the reasons that veal leg (most commonly served in thick osso buco slices) has a similarly pleasing mouthfeel.

Cooking a whole bone-in leg high above a strong fire produces a delicious swirl of wood smoke and flavorful steam (from the baste drippings, melted lamb fat, and meat juices). I find this to be one of the best lullabies on earth. Just at that point when I feel I could nod off, the sound of a tsst! of steam will stop me and I get back to the business of active grilling.

Slowly the flavorful crust builds up, and finishing by rapid cooking and basting at the end, when you lower the meat so that it is closer to the flame, produces the ultimate herbaceous, crispy crust.

Gotta have a chewy full-bodied red wine with this!

One 6½-pound bone-in leg of lamb, aitchbone removed (you can have the butcher do this), trimmed, and tied every 2 inches with kitchen string

6 tablespoons Four Seasons Blend (page 7)

2 tablespoons coarsely ground black pepper

An herb brush (see page 8)

2 cups baste of your choice (pages 230–34, made with the acid component)

Board Dressing (page 27)

- Set up the grill with an elevated grate (see page 59) and preheat it to high.

- Season the leg of lamb all over with the seasoning blend and pepper, then lightly moisten your hands with water and work the seasonings into the meat. Allow to stand for 10 minutes to develop a "meat paste" (see page 8).

- Put the lamb on the clean (unoiled) grill grate and cook, without moving it, for 4 minutes. Roll the lamb a quarter turn and cook for 4 minutes, then turn the lamb again and repeat until you've cooked it for 4 minutes each on all four sides. The meat may stick and tear a bit, but this is OK, even desirable—the sticking and tearing is what I call "meat scruffing" (see page 8). (For newer grills, where less sticking and tearing occurs, or for increased surface area, score with a knife—see page 14.)

- Give the lamb a quarter turn, baste with the herb brush, and continue cooking, rolling the lamb a quarter turn every 4 minutes (see The Hot Potato Method, page 24) and basting each time the meat is moved, until the internal temperature registers 115°F on an instant-read thermometer, 10 to 15 minutes longer.

- Transfer the lamb to a platter, brush lightly with the baste, and let rest for at least 10 minutes, and up to 30 minutes.

- Meanwhile, carefully remove the elevated grill grate.

- Put the lamb on the hot grill and cook, turning every 3 or 4 minutes and basting lightly every time the lamb is moved, until the internal temperature registers 135°F.

- Meanwhile, pour the board dressing onto a cutting board (or mix it directly on the board). Finely chop the tip of the herb brush and mix the herbs into the dressing.

- Transfer the lamb to the cutting board and roll it in the dressing to coat. Allow to rest for 10 to 15 minutes.

- To serve, carve the meat into ¼-inch-thick slices, turning each slice in the dressing to coat, and arrange on plates. Pour some of the board juices over each serving.

CLINCHING:
DOWN AND DIRTY

I don't know of many cooking techniques that were inspired by boxing, but this one is. If you are any kind of fighter at all and you are going up against an opponent who has a longer reach—i.e., has longer arms than you do—the only strategy that will serve you in the long run is "to close the gap." In other words, you have to eliminate that advantage by getting closer to your opponent's body so that the difference in reach is not a factor. Often this means you are "clinching," or hanging on with both arms, waiting for an opportunity when your opponent tries to step back and leaves you an opening, so you can deliver a knockout blow.

Cooking meat is not the same kind of physical combat as prize fighting, to be sure, but there are winners and losers in this arena as well. One of the greatest challenges of good crust development and thorough, even cooking is flare-up. When meat fat catches fire, it can leave an acrid slick that even the choicest cut of perfectly seasoned meat cannot overcome.

Through a lucky accident, I discovered that flame can sometimes be an ally rather than an obstacle. I was in Iowa cooking a ton of pork shoulders at a special event. When I checked on my meat, I felt it needed more "aroma therapy." Normally I would have thrown some pork scraps into the firebox of my offset smoker, but I didn't have any scraps, and the train (that is to say, the pork) had already left the station. What I did have was a nice fatty extra shoulder, so I put the whole shoulder into the firebox. This is not something I would ever recommend with a great cut of meat, but in this situation, I had to use what was at hand.

About two hours later, I was really hungry—no wonder, with the tantalizing perfume of all that pork cooking. In desperation, I opened the firebox and instead of finding a charred cinder, my "aromatizing" pork shoulder looked beautiful. And it tasted just as good: crispy, crackling, and moist.

Hmm . . .

By "cooking dirty," I mean cooking directly on the coals, having first cleared any coating of ash by using a hair dryer.

I thought about what had happened. I had expected a carbonized hunk of inedible meat, but then I realized that if you "close the gap" between the meat and the coals, there is no room for flame. Instead, the heat is transferred directly, and instantly, into the meat and any flames are smothered. Instead of a long process of building up the crust, this alternative superheats any melting fat, basting ingredients, and juices and penetrates the meat with a blast of aromatized steam.

There are two ways that you can use the clinching method. The first one is hard-core and gets a lot of comments from grillside backseat drivers. I call it "cooking dirty" or "coals direct and all that comes with it," by which I mean cooking directly on the coals, after clearing them of any coating of ash by using a hair dryer or fanning them with a big piece of stiff cardboard. After cooking, I flick off any remaining ash from the cooked meat before serving. (Personally, though, I kind of like a little bit of burnt ash, almost as a seasoning. You will be surprised at how little ash there is.)

If you are ash-o-phobic, however, or have a lot of meat to cook, you can get the same clinching effect by cooking "clean on the screen," placing a thin grill or grate (such as a wire cooling rack) directly on the coals. It closes the gap without putting the meat directly in contact with the ash, and it's less work to flick off the ash.

In either case, this can be done only with lump charcoal, not briquettes.

The meat is placed so close to the coals that the transfer of heat is direct and there is no space for acrid flame buildup.

92   Clinched Strip Steak
A "New York strip" cooked
on the coals for an intense
blast of superheated flavor.

98   Clinched Beef Tenderloin
How to get the most flavor and
tenderness out of tenderloin.

100 Clinched Boneless Pork Chops
As tender as the best pork
chop you can remember
from childhood.

**102 Clinched Double-Wide
Loin Lamb Chops**
Cooks quickly, gives you a
beautiful crust and, on the
inside, *à point* lamb.

104 Clinched Chicken Wingettes
Wings that are just as crispy
as those served at happy hour
in a great bar, but with deep
chicken flavor.

PREPARING A MATURE AND LEVEL BED OF COALS

When cooking on coals, it is important to even them out, lightly tamping them down to a uniform height of 4 to 6 inches. A cast-iron skillet or a roasting pan will serve you well for this task. Then, just before placing the meat on the coals (or grate), use a hair dryer or a piece of cardboard to fan the coals sufficiently to clear away bits of ash.

The clinching method works best
for cuts with a smoother muscle
surface, such as rump, New York strip,
or tenderloin. And it is best suited
for cuts that are cooked to rare or
medium-rare. The exception is items
needing to be extremely well cooked,
such as chicken legs.

CLINCHED STRIP STEAK

Serves 4

Marbled, full-flavored strip steak is what most people have in mind when they think of the classic steak. Even a thousand miles from Manhattan, the cut is often referred to as a New York strip, bringing to mind the era of the speakeasy, free-spending gangsters in loud pinstripe suits, big jazz bands, and cigarette girls walking among the tables in heels and revealing outfits.

The atomization produced when the fat and juices from the marbled meat make contact with the hot coals creates an intense blast of superheated flavor that infuses meat, fish, or fowl.

When cooked medium-rare, these steaks take only 9 minutes or so. In order to be able to properly time and manipulate them, I'd say four steaks is the limit that you can prepare at one time.

Four 10-ounce boneless strip steaks, at least 1¼ inches thick, fat trimmed to ¼ inch

¼ cup Four Seasons Blend (page 7)

An herb brush (see page 8)

½ cup Butter Baste (page 234)

Board Dressing (page 27)

Finishing Salt of your choice (pages 244–53) or sea or kosher salt

- Allow the steaks to come to room temperature, approximately 1 hour if straight from the refrigerator.

- Prepare a "mature and level" coal bed (see page 90), with a clean thin grate or rack set over it if you like; the fire should be very hot.

- Season the steaks on both sides with the seasoning blend, then lightly moisten your hands with water and work the seasonings into the meat. Allow to stand for 5 minutes to develop a "meat paste" (see page 8).

- Fan or blow-dry excess ash from the coal fire (see photos, page 90).

- Using the herb brush, brush the steaks lightly with the butter baste. Put them on the grill grate or directly on the coals and cook, without moving them, for 2 minutes. Turn the steaks, baste lightly, and cook for 2 minutes, then repeat two more times, basting the steaks each time they are flipped.

- Lean the steaks up against one another, on their sides, fat side down, and cook for 1 minute. Repeat on the other side (two sides in total), until the steaks reach an internal temperature of 110° to 115°F.

- Meanwhile, pour the board dressing onto a cutting board (or mix it directly on the board). Finely chop the tip of the herb brush and mix the herbs into the dressing.

- Transfer the steaks to the cutting board and turn them in the dressing to coat. Allow to rest for 5 minutes.

- To serve, slice the steaks ½ inch thick, turning each slice in the dressing to coat, and arrange on plates. Pour some of the board juices over each serving and finish with a sprinkling of the salt.

Don't worry when you grill food directly on the coals—the ash will not interfere with the meat. It's so hot that it doesn't leave any residue you can taste, nor does it affect the texture of the finished meat.

CLINCHED BONELESS PORK CHOPS

Serves 6

There are few eternal verities in cooking, but surely one of them must be that pork chops are perennially dry. Here is another solution to the problem (see also Thick Pork Chops, Guaranteed Juicy, page 76). Cooking the chops quickly to rosy pinkness ensures that the relatively unmarbled flesh stays moist and tender.

With clinching, your goal is to get the meat done and onto the plate quickly. You don't want carryover cooking. You do want quick, even heating. A clinched boneless pork chop cooks evenly and uniformly and the result is juicy and tender.

Six 8- to 10-ounce boneless pork loin chops, at least 2 inches thick

Basic Brine (page 238) or 8 cups Very Basic Brine (page 238)

3 tablespoons Four Seasons Blend (page 7)

An herb brush (see page 8)

½ cup Butter Baste (page 234)

Board Dressing (page 27)

- Put the pork chops in a heavy-duty plastic bag or a medium bowl and add the brine. Seal the bag or cover the bowl and refrigerate for at least 12 hours, and up to 16 hours.

- Drain the pork chops (discard the brine) and pat dry with paper towels. Allow to come to room temperature, approximately 1 hour.

- Prepare a "mature and level" coal bed (see page 90), with a clean thin grate or rack set over it if you like; the fire should be very hot.

- Season the pork chops on both sides with the seasoning blend, then lightly moisten your hands with water and work the seasonings into the meat. Allow to stand for 5 minutes to develop a "meat paste" (see page 8).

- Fan or blow-dry excess ash from the coal fire (see photos, page 90).

- Using the herb brush, brush the pork chops lightly all over with the butter baste. Put the pork chops on the grill grate or directly on the coals and cook, without moving them, for 2 minutes. Turn the chops, baste lightly, and cook for 2 minutes, then repeat two more times, basting the chops each time they are flipped.

- Lean the pork chops up against one another, fat side down, and cook for 1 minute, or until the internal temperature registers 135°F on an instant-read thermometer.

- Meanwhile, pour the board dressing onto a cutting board (or mix it directly on the board). Finely chop the tip of the herb brush and mix the herbs into the dressing.

- Transfer the pork chops to the cutting board and turn them in the dressing to coat. Allow to rest for 5 minutes.

- To serve, arrange the pork chops on plates and pour some of the board juices over each one.

CLINCHED DOUBLE-WIDE LOIN LAMB CHOPS

Serves 8 to 10

When Pete and I tried this in London, we were amazed. It's probably what made us decide to do a whole chapter on clinching. Lamb that doesn't flare up, leaving a slick black residue, is the Holy Grail of every lamb griller. You can cook these chops quickly, with no flame, to produce a beautiful crust and, on the inside, *à point* (perfect) lamb.

For the most part I avoid clinching with bone-in pieces, but here the bone doesn't affect the cooking at all—it's essentially just a way of holding the two loin sections together, which makes for a different presentation from a typical lamb chop. You'll need to get these chops from a specialty butcher.

This cut—two sections of loin joined by a bone—is called a Barnsley chop in England and an English chop among old-time American butchers.

Eight to ten 8- to 10-ounce English-cut lamb chops (also called double loin chops), 1½ inches thick, fat trimmed to ¼ inch

3 tablespoons Four Seasons Blend (page 7)

An herb brush (see page 8)

½ cup Butter Baste (page 234)

Board Dressing (page 27)

A clean brick, wrapped in foil

- Allow the lamb to come to room temperature, approximately 1 hour if straight from the refrigerator.

- Prepare a "mature and level" coal bed (see page 90), with a clean thin grate or rack set over it if you like; the fire should be very hot.

- Season the lamb chops on both sides with the seasoning blend, then lightly moisten your hands with water and work the seasonings into the meat. Allow to stand for 5 minutes to develop a "meat paste" (see page 8).

- Fan or blow-dry excess ash from the coal fire (see photos, page 90).

- Using the herb brush, brush the chops lightly all over with the butter baste. Put the lamb chops on the grill grate or directly on the coals and cook, without moving them, for 3 minutes. Turn, baste lightly, and cook for 3 minutes, then repeat, basting each time the chops are flipped.

- Put the foil-wrapped brick on the grill grate or on the coals to be used as a steady point for the chops, lean the chops up against it, fat side down, and cook for 1 minute, or until the internal temperature registers 120°F on an instant-read thermometer.

- Meanwhile, pour the board dressing onto a cutting board (or mix it directly on the board). Finely chop the tip of the herb brush and mix the herbs into the dressing.

- Transfer the lamb chops to the cutting board and turn in the dressing to coat, then transfer to plates and serve.

CLINCHED CHICKEN WINGETTES

Serves 8 to 10

Usually served with heavily flavored sauces, chicken wings are often regarded as just an easy-to-pick-up medium for dipping. But, as I found when I visited my father, who lives in Thailand, wings can be cooked quickly on a robata grill (see Sources, page 256) or a hibachi-style grill, and they are just as crispy as the deep-fried wings that are standard bar fare in the United States. The advantage is you highlight rather than obscure the flavor of chicken.

24 to 30 chicken wingettes (wing pieces, not including wing tips)

Basic Brine (page 238) or 8 cups Very Basic Brine (page 238)

6 tablespoons Four Seasons Blend (page 7)

1 cup Butter Baste (page 234)

An herb brush (see page 8)

¼ cup chopped fresh chives

Finishing Salt of your choice (pages 244–53) or sea or kosher salt

- Put the wings in a large heavy-duty plastic bag or a medium bowl and add the brine. Seal the bag or cover the bowl and refrigerate for at least 12 hours, and up to 16 hours.

- Drain the chicken wings (discard the brine) and pat lightly dry with paper towels. Allow to come to room temperature, approximately 30 minutes.

- Prepare a "mature and level" coal bed (see page 90), with a clean thin grate or rack set over it if desired; the fire should be very hot.

- Season the wings all over with the seasoning blend, then lightly moisten your hands with water and work the seasonings into the wings. Let stand for 5 minutes to develop a "meat paste" (see page 8).

- Fan or blow-dry excess ash from the coal fire (see photos, page 90).

- Toss the wings with the butter baste in a large bowl and arrange in a single layer in a grill basket; reserve the butter baste in the bowl. Put the basket on the grill grate or directly on the coals and cook for 3 minutes. Turn the basket, baste the wings with the herb brush, and cook for 3 minutes, then repeat two more times, basting each time the basket is flipped.

- Transfer the basket to a platter and allow the wings (still inside the basket) to rest for 5 minutes.

- Put the basket back on the grill grate or coals and cook for 2 minutes, then flip over and cook for 2 minutes, or until the wings are crispy and cooked through.

- Remove the chicken from the grill and carefully open the basket, teasing off any pieces that have stuck. Transfer to a platter, sprinkle with the chives and salt, and serve.

CLINCHED AND PLANKED

I have always liked the idea of planked food, but it wasn't until I came up with the clinching technique (see Clinching: Down and Dirty, page 84) and then combined it with plank cooking that I felt I had broken through with something truly special. It is one of my favorite things that has come out of writing this book.

The first time I saw planking was during my time as a student at the Culinary Institute of America. We were deeply immersed in the complexities of Escoffier and the classic sauces of haute cuisine.

But then a Native American chef from the Northwest came to give my class a lecture on planking fish. It was so simple. He described how to make the fire, put a piece of salmon on a board, and prop it up so that it faces the fire at a distance that makes for the optimum cooking temperature. The result was delicious and appealing to me because of its simplicity. As I considered that salmon in the context of the canon of French cuisine, I came to the conclusion that has stayed with me ever since: whether complex or simple, "Flavor rules!"

By briefly clinching your meat, fish, or fowl, you develop a quick crust. Then, by transferring it to a presoaked plank and cooking it covered, you get a uniform tempering effect from the plank, while the flavorful smoky steam permeates the meat. Here the process is so quick that it's all about accelerated development of crust, flavor, and even tempering. As with many things in life, once I got over my planking prejudice, I started to discover how well it works with and without clinching.

Apart from its virtues in cooking and flavoring, planking adds beautiful color to the crust. Different woods impart different flavors and colors. Fruitwoods are lovely. I use cedar and oak here because they are readily available in cooking supply stores. If you don't want to spend the extra dollars for these planks, which are prepared especially for cooking, you can economize with wood from the lumberyard. The planks I use are 6 inches by 12 inches. *Please make sure that you use raw, untreated timber!*

I serve these recipes directly from the plank. It looks really good. You will, of course, need to put the plank on another board or platter to protect your table from the heat.

110 Clinched-and-Planked Shrimp
An ultra-quick starter for
a barbecue.

**114 Clinched-and-Planked
Lobster Tails**
Split tails mean lots of meat
and no wrestling with drippy,
hard-to-crack shells.

**116 Clinched-and-Planked
Rump Steaks**
New life for an old cut of
beef: more toothsome than
a filet and more flavorful.

**118 Clinched-and-Planked
Lamb Racks**
A fruitwood plank lets the
lamb pick up the subtle flavor
and an earthy perfume.

**122 Clinched-and-Planked
Game Steaks**
A lean cut with a quick,
flavorful crust and a
juicy interior.

**124 Clinched-and-Planked
Chicken Legs**
Get mouthwatering dark
meat without incinerating
the outside of your chicken.

**128 Clinched-and-Planked
Duck Breasts**
Finally, here's how to
replicate a gorgeous tea-
smoked duck on the grill.

**130 Clinched-and-Planked
Fish Steaks**
Flaky perfection with
a restauranty crust.

CLINCHED-AND-PLANKED SHRIMP

Serves 8

Shrimp on the barbie, as the Australians say, can be superb. Just as often, though, it can be dry and tough. Cooking it in the shell, tempering it with the wet plank, and evenly transferring heat through steam rising off the plank means the delicate shrimp proteins are triple-protected. Because they can be cooked and served in a matter of minutes, these shrimp are a great starter at a barbecue.

16 jumbo shrimp (6–8 per pound)

Basic Brine (page 238) or Very Basic Brine (page 238)

2 cups baste of your choice (pages 230–34, made with the acid component)

2 tablespoons freshly squeezed lemon juice

2 tablespoons extra virgin olive oil

¼ cup ½-inch batons fresh chives

1 untreated plank, soaked in water for 1 hour

- Split the shrimp shells down the back and devein the shrimp, leaving the shells intact. Put the shrimp in a large heavy-duty plastic bag or a medium bowl and add the brine. Seal the bag or cover the bowl and refrigerate for 1 hour.

- Prepare a "mature and level" coal bed (see page 90); the fire should be very hot.

- Drain the shrimp (discard the brine) and pat lightly dry with paper towels. Toss with the baste in a large bowl, coating well, then line 8 shrimp up in 2 rows. Arrange the remaining shrimp curled inside the first ones (see photo).

- Put the plank on the coal bed with some coals on the exposed corners of the plank and then cover with a grill lid, a large metal bowl, or a domed lid. Cook and smoke for 6 to 8 minutes, until the shrimp are opaque throughout and pearly looking.

- Transfer the shrimp to a platter, toss with the lemon juice, olive oil, and chives, and serve.

Using a dome (opposite) creates an oven-like effect and captures smoky flavor.

CLINCHED-AND-PLANKED LOBSTER TAILS

Serves 8

While it is true that almost everybody loves lobster, it is equally true that few people like the inevitable cleanup that goes with whole lobster. Split tails get you right to the heart of the matter—lots of meat and no wrestling with drippy, hard-to-crack shells. The shells actually serve a culinary purpose: they preserve moisture and give the meat a deep toasted flavor. (In classic French cooking, we always saved the shells from shrimp, prawns, crabs, and lobsters, roasting them and using them in sauces.) Save the claws and other meaty parts for salads or another dish.

For this recipe, please start with live lobsters, or you run the risk of an unpleasant ammonia-type aroma. I find the most effective and humane way to kill lobsters is with a strong thrust of a chef's knife to the head, which will dispatch them immediately.

8 lobster tails, split lengthwise in half

2 tablespoons Four Seasons Blend (page 7)

2 cups baste of your choice (pages 230–34, made with the acid component)

2 tablespoons freshly squeezed lemon juice

2 tablespoons extra virgin olive oil

¼ cup ½-inch batons fresh chives

4 untreated planks, soaked in water for 1 hour

• Prepare a "mature and level" coal bed (see page 90); the fire should be hot.

• Season the lobster tails with the seasoning blend, rubbing it into the meat. Toss the lobster with the baste in a large bowl until well coated, then arrange 4 half tails side by side on each plank (see upper-right photo, opposite).

• Put the planks on the coal bed with some coals on the exposed corners of the planks and then cover with a grill lid, a large metal bowl, or a domed lid. Cook and smoke for 12 to 15 minutes, until the lobster meat is opaque throughout.

• Remove shells, transfer the lobster to a platter, toss with the lemon juice, olive oil, and chives, and serve.

For a cool-looking presentation, notch
both ends of the lobster tail and then
fit them together to form a circle.

CLINCHED-AND-PLANKED RUMP STEAKS

Serves 8

Like the filet, the rump is a lump of muscle without a lot of marbling. This means you must be vigilant about not overcooking it. It is more toothsome than filet mignon and more flavorful, if no less forgiving in the cooking process. Cedar-clinching is ideal because it is fast, so the meat isn't overcooked and, at the same time, the steam from the board really infuses the flavor.

Eight 8- to 10-ounce rump steaks, 1½ to 2 inches thick

¼ cup Four Seasons Blend (page 7)

An herb brush (see page 8)

2 cups baste of your choice (pages 230–34; reserve the acid component to add later)

Board Dressing (page 27)

Finishing Salt of your choice (pages 244–53) or sea or kosher salt

4 untreated planks, soaked in water for 1 hour

• Allow the rump steaks to come to room temperature.

• Prepare a "mature and level" coal bed (see page 90), with a clean thin grate or rack set over it if you like; the fire should be very hot.

• Season the steaks on both sides with the seasoning blend, then lightly moisten your hands with water and rub the seasonings into the meat. Allow to stand for 5 minutes to develop a "meat paste" (see page 8).

• Using the herb brush, moisten the steaks on all sides with the fat portion of the baste. Put the steaks on the grill grate or directly on the coals and cook, without moving them, for 1 minute. Turn the steaks, baste lightly, and cook for another minute, then repeat two more times, basting the steaks lightly each time they are flipped. Transfer the steaks to a platter and baste them generously.

- Add the acid to the remaining baste. Remove the grill grate, if you used it. Baste the steaks and arrange 2 steaks side by side on each plank. Put the planks on the coal bed with some coals on the exposed corners of the planks and then cover with a grill lid, a large metal bowl, or a domed lid. Cook and smoke until the internal temperature registers 115°F on an instant-read thermometer, about 5 minutes.

- Meanwhile, pour the board dressing onto a cutting board (or mix it directly on the board). Finely chop the tip of the herb brush and mix the herbs into the dressing.

- Transfer the steaks to the cutting board and allow to rest for 3 minutes.

- To serve, slice the steaks, turning each slice in the dressing to coat, and arrange on plates. Finish with a sprinkling of the salt.

CLINCHED-AND-PLANKED LAMB RACKS

Serves 8

As anyone who has handed a credit card over to the butcher when buying a bunch of lamb racks knows, the total can look like the down payment for a mortgage. Because they are so expensive, be sure to take as much care as you can in the cooking. Like a beef fillet, this cut should only be served medium-rare, or it will be tough and dry. Although you don't get the multiple textures and states of doneness that is one of the pleasures of leg of lamb, there is a little eye right next to the bone that is fatty, chewy, and unctuous.

Because lamb is so rich and flavorful, when I can get it, I like to use fruitwood for the plank so the lamb picks up a subtle but flavorful perfume from the steam rising out of the wood.

Four 7- or 8-bone lamb racks (about 1¼ pounds each), cut in half and frenched (you can have the butcher do this)

¼ cup Four Seasons Blend (page 7)

An herb brush (see page 8)

4 cups baste of your choice (pages 230–34; reserve the acid component to add later)

Board Dressing (page 27)

Finishing Salt of your choice (pages 244–53) or sea or kosher salt

4 untreated planks, soaked in water for 1 hour

- Allow the lamb to come to room temperature (about 1 hour if straight from the refrigerator).

- Prepare a "mature and level" coal bed (see page 90), with a clean thin grate or rack set over it if you like; the fire should be very hot.

- Season the lamb all over with the seasoning blend, then lightly moisten your hands with water and work the seasonings into the meat and fat. Allow to stand for 5 minutes to develop a "meat paste" (see page 8).

- Using the herb brush, moisten the racks on all sides with the fat portion of the baste. Put the lamb racks fat side down on the grill grate or directly on the coals and cook, without moving them, for 2 minutes. Turn them over, baste lightly, and cook for 2 minutes, then repeat two more times, basting the racks each time they are flipped. Transfer to a platter and baste generously.

• Add the acid to the fat baste. Remove the grill grate, if you used it. Baste the lamb and put 2 half racks on each plank, leaning the racks against each other, bone end up, like a teepee (see photo). Put the planks on the coal bed with some coals on the exposed corners of the planks and then cover with a grill lid, a large metal bowl, or a domed lid. Cook and smoke until the internal temperature registers 125°F on an instant-read thermometer, turning the racks around once, about 8 minutes.

• Meanwhile, pour the board dressing onto a cutting board (or mix it directly on the board). Finely chop the tip of the herb brush and mix the herbs into the dressing.

• Transfer the racks to the cutting board and allow to rest for 3 minutes.

• To serve, slice the racks into individual chops, turning each one in the dressing to coat, and arrange on plates. Pour some of the board juices over each serving and finish with a sprinkling of the salt.

By cooking right next to the coals, basting, and then creating more smoke with your planks, the lamb picks up a maximum of smoky, herbaceous flavor.

CLINCHED-AND-PLANKED
GAME STEAKS

Serves 8

Game, especially wild game (as opposed to farm-raised animals), is lean meat: deep flavor, but so lean that, like a rack of lamb or a filet mignon, it shouldn't be served past medium-rare. Robustly basting with fat baste during clinching creates a quick, flavorful crust, and then the smoky steam from the plank infuses the meat without drying it out.

There is nothing more primevally special and satisfying to me as a chef than to have a hunter bring in his trophy and ask me to prepare it.

Eight 8- to 10-ounce boneless game steaks (venison, elk, antelope, etc.), 1½ to 2 inches thick

¼ cup Four Seasons Blend (page 7)

An herb brush (see page 8)

2 cups baste of your choice (pages 230–34; reserve the acid component to add later)

Board Dressing (page 27)

Finishing Salt of your choice (pages 244–53) or sea or kosher salt

4 untreated planks, soaked in water for 1 hour

• Allow the game to come to room temperature.

• Prepare a "mature and level" coal bed (see page 90), with a clean thin grate or rack set over it if desired; the fire should be very hot.

• Season the game steaks on both sides with the seasoning blend, then lightly moisten your hands with water and work the seasonings into the meat. Allow to stand for 5 minutes to develop a "meat paste" (see page 8).

• Using the herb brush, moisten the steaks on all sides with the fat portion of the baste. Put the steaks on the grill grate or directly on the coals and cook, without moving, for 1 minute. Turn over, baste lightly, and cook for 1 minute, then repeat two more times, basting each time.

- Transfer the steaks to a platter, baste generously, and flip over. Allow to rest for 5 minutes.

- Add the acid to the fat baste. Remove the grill grate, if you used it. Baste the steaks and place 2 steaks side by side on each plank. Put the planks on the coal bed with some coals on the exposed corners of the planks and then cover with a grill lid, a large metal bowl, or a domed lid. Cook and smoke until the internal temperature registers 115° to 120°F on an instant-read thermometer, about 5 minutes.

- Meanwhile, pour the board dressing onto a cutting board (or mix it directly on the board). Finely chop the tip of the herb brush and mix the herbs into the dressing.

- Transfer the steaks to the cutting board and allow to rest for 3 minutes.

- To serve, slice the steaks ½ inch thick, turning each slice in the dressing to coat, and arrange on plates. Finish with a sprinkling of the salt.

CLINCHED-AND-PLANKED CHICKEN LEGS

Serves 8

Because of its depth of flavor, dark-meat chicken clearly wins out over easy-to-dry-out white meat. It also has more intramuscular fat and more collagen. The result is juicier, more mouthwatering meat. But one of the problems that often confronts the chicken griller is that by the time the dark meat is cooked through, the outside is incinerated. Quick-clinching, however, sets the crust and begins the rapid transfer of heat into the meat, and then the superheated steam from the plank finishes the job. Don't misunderstand me—I have nothing against white meat, as in a perfectly roasted chicken—but in the world of barbecue, dark meat is my favorite!

8 whole chicken legs, each one slashed to the bone in a few places (see photo, page 127)

Basic Brine (page 238) or 8 cups Very Basic Brine (page 238)

2 tablespoons Four Seasons Blend (page 7)

An herb brush (see page 8)

2 cups baste of your choice (pages 230–34; reserve the acid component to add later)

Board Dressing (page 27)

¼ cup fresh tarragon leaves, chopped with a few passes of the knife

Finishing Salt of your choice (pages 244–53) or sea or kosher salt

4 untreated planks, soaked in water for 1 hour

• Put the chicken legs in a large heavy-duty plastic bag or a large bowl and add the brine. Seal the bag or cover the bowl and refrigerate for 3 hours.

• Drain the chicken (discard the brine) and pat lightly dry with paper towels. Allow to come to room temperature, approximately 30 minutes.

• Prepare a "mature and level" coal bed (see page 90), with a clean thin grate or rack set over it if you like; the fire should be very hot.

• Season the chicken legs all over with the seasoning blend, then lightly moisten your hands with water and work the seasonings into the chicken. Allow to stand for 5 minutes to develop a "meat paste" (see page 8).

CONTINUED

- Moisten the chicken legs on all sides with the fat portion of the baste. Put the chicken legs skin side down on the grill grate or directly on the coals and cook, without moving them, for 2 minutes. Turn them, baste lightly, and cook for 2 minutes, then repeat two more times, basting the chicken each time it is flipped.

- Transfer the chicken legs to a platter, skin side up, and baste generously. Allow to rest for 5 minutes.

- Add the acid to the fat baste. Remove the grill grate, if you used it. Baste the chicken legs and put 2 legs side by side on each plank. Put the planks on the coal bed with some coals on the exposed corners of the planks and then cover with a grill lid, a large metal bowl, or a domed lid. Cook and smoke for 10 to 12 minutes, or until the juices run clear when a chicken thigh is pierced with a fork.

- Meanwhile, pour the board dressing onto a cutting board (or mix it directly on the board). Finely chop the tip of the herb brush and mix the herbs into the dressing.

- Transfer the chicken legs to the cutting board, turning them in the dressing to coat, then turn skin side up. Sprinkle with the tarragon and allow to rest for 3 minutes.

- To serve, arrange the chicken on plates and finish with a sprinkling of the salt.

In the first photo, I'm slashing the chicken to the bone in a few places. Cutting before cooking doesn't dry out the meat.

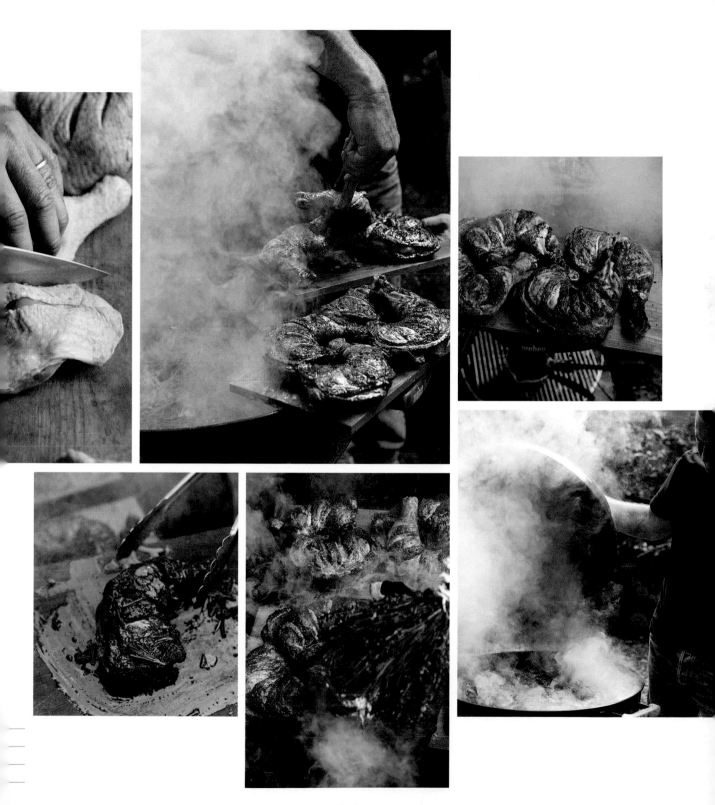

CLINCHED-AND-PLANKED DUCK BREASTS

Serves 8

Duck, like lamb, presents a problem for the griller. The superhigh amount of fat in the skin has a tendency to flame up intensely, potentially leaving a greasy residue on the meat. Simple clinching doesn't help much, because by the time the skin has crisped, the interior is still close to raw. Cedar-clinching is the solution. First you clinch the duck for a few minutes to crisp the skin and build flavor with a baste, and then you transfer the duck breast to a prepped plank to finish cooking. The smoldering smoke from the board infuses the duck and continues to transfer well-tempered heat to the interior. The color of the planked skin is gorgeous, just like the tea-smoked duck that they showed us how to make in culinary school. I'd always wanted to duplicate that wonderful texture and flavor using a barbecue. Finally, success!

Eight 8- to 10-ounce magrets (boneless duck breast halves)

¼ cup Four Seasons Blend (page 7)

An herb brush (see page 8)

2 cups baste of your choice (pages 230–34; reserve the acid component to add later)

Board Dressing (page 27)

¼ cup finely chopped fresh chives

Finishing Salt of your choice (pages 244–53) or sea or kosher salt

4 untreated planks, soaked in water for 1 hour

- Prepare a "mature and level" coal bed (see page 90), with a clean thin grate or rack set over it if you like; the fire should be very hot.

- Season the duck breasts all over with the seasoning blend, then lightly moisten your hands with water and work the seasonings into the breasts. Allow to stand for 5 minutes to develop a "meat paste" (see page 8).

- Using the herb brush, moisten the duck breasts on both sides with the fat portion of the baste. Put the breasts fat side down on the grill grate or directly on the coals and cook, without moving them, for 3 minutes. Turn them, baste lightly, and cook for 3 minutes, then repeat two more times, basting the duck each time it is moved. Transfer the duck to a platter and baste generously.

- Add the acid to the fat baste. Remove the grill grate, if you used it. Baste the duck and arrange 2 breasts side by side, skin side up, on each plank. Put the planks on the coal bed with some coals on the exposed corners of the planks and then cover with a grill lid, a large metal bowl, or a domed lid. Cook and smoke until the internal temperature registers 115° to 120°F on an instant-read thermometer, about 4 minutes.

- Meanwhile, pour the board dressing onto a cutting board (or mix it directly on the board). Finely chop the tip of the herb brush and mix the herbs into the dressing.

- Transfer the duck to the cutting board, fat side up, and and allow to rest for 3 minutes.

- To serve, slice the duck breasts, turning each slice in the dressing to coat, and arrange on plates. Finish with a sprinkling of the chives and salt.

Part III

CO-STARS

A shared meal strengthens family bonds, cements friendships, repairs enmities, establishes sacred communion. Fire, food, family, friendship: they all go together. Just like Thanksgiving and Academy Award night, barbecue meals are meant for a group of family or friends to gather and bond.

But few books or menus seriously consider the question "Isn't the company you provide for the meat, fish, or fowl on the plate equally important to the success of the meal?" Instead, most people spend hours getting the main course ready, then pile on the baked beans, potato salad, coleslaw, etc. at the last minute and leave it at that. The side dishes are usually an afterthought, but I suggest we get rid of the term "side dish" and talk about "co-stars." A first-rate barbecue dinner requires that equal care and skill be given to everything that is served with the meat.

Think about what's normally on your plate at a typical barbecue. How do you approach it? Let's say that you have some pulled pork, some coleslaw, and some baked beans. Nobody starts by eating all the meat and, when that is done, eating all the beans and then polishing off the coleslaw. You push some meat onto your fork, then a few sweet and hearty beans and some crunchy, creamy coleslaw, and you taste all three at once. Contrasting tastes and textures make that forkful interesting.

You may recognize some of these co-stars as new approaches to old favorites, while others are my own inventions. One thing you will not find here is the dutiful "serve with" suggestion after each recipe. To my way of thinking, a plate with barbecue on it requires three items: you pick them. Just like my family did, way back when, at the Jade King Chinese restaurant in Roslyn, Long Island, take one from Group A (meat, fish, or fowl) and two from Group B (the co-stars). How you put together your ensemble depends on what you are in the mood for. Satisfying spontaneous desire is a much better route than satisfying the instructions in a one-combination-fits-all cookbook suggestion.

It goes without saying that these recipes don't exhaust all the co-star variations you can serve at a barbecue, but the principles behind each group can lead to endless variations. As chefs do, let the best items in the markets work on your imagination, and then start chopping and slicing.

MELTING, CREAMY, AND COMFORTABLE

The big powerful flavors that are the goal of every griller can easily overwhelm your palate. I think that in order to fully appreciate the main dish, you need some contrasts in texture or temperature, something to smooth out the experience and comfort your palate. The smooth and creamy co-stars in this chapter calm down the strength of barbecue without getting in the way of flavor. In addition to tempering the mouthfeel of big brawny barbecue recipes, melting and creamy co-stars can add an unctuous quality that completes lean dishes such as fish or beef or pork tenderloin.

138 **Mushrooms in Parsley Cream**
A lesson from my grandpa.

140 **Creamed Corn with
Chives and Chiles**
Use Philadelphia cream
cheese as a thickener to
reinvent an old favorite.

142 **Bubbling Bacon Butter Beans**
Velvety, smoky, and creamy;
serve with anything, or nothing
at all!

144 **UKBB (United Kingdom
Baked Beans)**
When you want beans for
more than hot dogs.

146 **Smoked-Corn Flan**
The sweet and savory flavor
of summer's best corn with
a smoky custard feel.

148 **Scruffed Carbonara Potatoes**
Think gnocchi, but way easier
to make.

150 **Melting Potatoes**
Creamy, steaming potatoes.

152 **Potato Cream with Leeks,
Capers, and Avocado**
A potato stew with herbs
and avocados.

154 **Creamed Spinach with
Steeped and Smoked
Garlic Confit**
Melty confited garlic
and creamy spinach.

156 **Polenta with Mascarpone
and Rosemary**
Herbaceous and creamy,
with a light funk.

MUSHROOMS IN PARSLEY CREAM

Serves 6 to 8

All grandpas have a pet saying that they will repeat for their grandchildren at every opportunity. My grandpa, William B. Perry, was fond of telling us that parsley is good for the blood. Maybe it is. Kids didn't go running to Google to fact-check their grandparents then. As a result of Grandpa's edict, I ate a lot of parsley when I was growing up, and I didn't care for it very much. But that was then, and now I am a cook and I appreciate the flavor and texture of this green herb, especially the way it pairs up with anything that has that special "fifth taste" known as umami, which we find in mushrooms, a particularly fine partner for all kinds of meat. I think this happy pairing has something to do with the texture of cooked mushrooms: smooth and moist, just like the collagen in meat when it has been lovingly cooked for a long time at the right temperature.

Note the use of *beurre manié*—butter kneaded with flour. In my years at Le Cirque and Daniel, I don't recall ever seeing flour used in any savory dish. When I moved on to Chanterelle, the gifted David Waltuck used *beurre manié* like crazy. It adds enough "stick" to sauces to hold them together without overreducing. I have come to rely on it as my "fixer."

3 tablespoons unsalted butter

1 cup finely chopped shallots

2 garlic cloves, crushed and peeled

Sea or kosher salt and freshly ground white pepper

Juice of 1 lemon, or to taste

2 tablespoons dry white wine

6 cups small firm white button mushrooms

A sprig of fresh thyme

1 cup chicken stock or canned low-sodium broth

2 cups heavy cream

½ teaspoon thinly shaved frozen *beurre manié* (see Note)

2 tablespoons finely chopped fresh flat-leaf parsley

• Cut 2 tablespoons of the butter into ½-inch cubes and refrigerate. Heat the remaining 1 tablespoon butter in a 4-quart pot over medium heat until it bubbles gently. Add the shallots, garlic, and a pinch each of salt and white pepper and cook until the shallots are just translucent, 2 to 3 minutes.

- Add the lemon juice and white wine, raise the heat to medium, bring to a boil, and cook until most of the liquid has evaporated, 2 to 3 minutes. Add the mushrooms and thyme, stirring well, then add the chicken stock, bring to a boil, and cook until reduced by half.

- Add the cream, bring to a simmer, and cook for 2 minutes. Add the *beurre manié*, stirring until incorporated, and simmer very gently for 10 minutes, or until well thickened.

- Meanwhile, wrap the parsley in a double layer of cheesecloth, run under cold water, and squeeze dry (rinsing the parsley will leach out some of the chlorophyll and prevent it from giving the cream a greenish tinge).

- Taste the mushrooms and adjust the seasoning if necessary. Swirl in the cubed butter piece by piece until incorporated, then remove from the heat and stir in the parsley. Adjust the acidity with a little more lemon juice if necessary, and serve.

NOTE

To make *beurre manié,* blend ½ cup all-purpose flour with 8 tablespoons (1 stick) unsalted butter, softened. Transfer to an airtight container, or shape into a log and wrap in plastic wrap and then foil, and freeze until needed. The butter will keep for at least a month.

CREAMED CORN
WITH CHIVES AND CHILES

Serves 6 to 8

Employing cream cheese as a thickener is a surprising use of a familiar taste. People always smile when they figure out that the secret ingredient is something they have eaten and enjoyed their whole lives.

Using the well-known and fondly remembered is a great strategy for creating recipes that people are predisposed to like. It's a door that opens out onto the pleasure in other less familiar ingredients and combinations.

I was introduced to this use of cream cheese in my early days on the barbecue circuit. I always made it a point to stop in at every barbecue place wherever I went, and that was how I came upon a restaurant named Jack Stack in Kansas City, with superfriendly people and equally super creamed corn.

"I love it," I said, "creamy and tangy . . . ? Hmm, I know what it is, but I can't place it."

"Philly cream cheese," they answered.

Cream cheese, just like what we had with bagels and lox on Sundays at home on Long Island. I think I may have been the only person in that part of KC who had regularly—or ever—eaten bagels and lox. I was connected to that recipe in a nostalgic way.

As for the combination of chiles and corn: they are both Native American foods, as is barbecued meat.

4 tablespoons unsalted butter

½ cup finely diced Spanish onion

¼ cup finely diced red bell pepper

¼ cup finely diced green bell pepper

3 garlic cloves, crushed and peeled

1 teaspoon fresh thyme leaves

1 teaspoon fresh rosemary leaves

½ teaspoon cayenne pepper

Juice of 1 lemon, or to taste

1 cup chicken stock or canned low-sodium broth

4 cups corn kernels (from 7 to 8 ears)

1 cup heavy cream

4 ounces cream cheese

Sea or kosher salt and freshly ground white pepper

½ cup shredded mild cheddar cheese

2 tablespoons thinly sliced (on the bias) scallions

3 tablespoons thinly sliced mild red chile pepper, such as Anaheim

2 tablespoons finely chopped fresh chives

- Cut 2 tablespoons of the butter into ½-inch cubes and refrigerate. Heat the remaining 2 tablespoons butter in a medium saucepan over medium heat until it crackles. Add the onion, bell peppers, garlic, thyme, rosemary, and cayenne and cook, stirring occasionally, until the onion is just translucent, 3 to 4 minutes.

- Add the lemon juice, raise the heat to medium, and cook until most of the liquid has evaporated, about 1 minute. Add the chicken stock, bring to a boil, and cook until reduced by half.

- Add the corn kernels, bring to a simmer, and cook until tender, about 5 minutes.

- Meanwhile, bring the cream just to a boil in a small saucepan. Add the cream cheese and whisk gently until melted and smooth.

- Add the cream mixture to the corn and stir gently until thoroughly incorporated, then simmer very gently for 3 to 4 minutes, stirring constantly. Season with salt and white pepper to taste, then swirl in the cubed butter piece by piece until incorporated. Stir in the shredded cheese.

- Remove from the heat and stir in the scallions, chile, and chives. Add more lemon juice and/or salt and pepper to taste and serve.

BUBBLING BACON BUTTER BEANS

Serves 6 to 8

Butter beans are just another name for lima beans, especially in the South. But I tend to think more sensually, and I have always felt that when they are cooked just right, these beans achieve a state of melty smoothness that is best described by the word "buttery." In the process of cooking, they throw off starch—just like Arborio rice does in risotto. The result is velvety creaminess. My recommendation for these beans is "Serve with anything," because they go with everything. But I could also say, "Serve with nothing else," because they are satisfying all by themselves and quite irresistible when you take them from the fire—steaming, bubbling, and fragrant.

3 tablespoons extra virgin olive oil, plus additional for drizzling

6 slices thick-sliced bacon, cut into ¼-inch-wide strips

½ cup finely chopped shallots

4 garlic cloves, crushed and peeled, plus 1 tablespoon grated garlic (use a Microplane) or garlic mashed to a paste

1 tablespoon chopped fresh sage

2 cups chicken stock or canned low-sodium broth

4 cups cooked butter beans or two 15-ounce jars or cans butter beans, drained, rinsed if canned

1 cup Pomì diced tomatoes (or other Tetra Pak tomatoes), drained

1 teaspoon dried oregano

¼ cup finely diced prosciutto fat (or additional bacon)

Sea or kosher salt and freshly ground black pepper

2 tablespoons finely chopped fresh flat-leaf parsley

White wine vinegar

• Preheat the oven to 300°F.

• Heat 2 tablespoons of the olive oil in a large saucepan over medium heat until it sizzles when a piece of bacon is added. Add the rest of the bacon, the shallots, crushed garlic, and sage and cook, stirring, until the shallots are just translucent, 3 to 4 minutes.

• Add the chicken stock and bring to a boil. Add the beans, bring to a simmer, and simmer for 10 minutes.

• Meanwhile, heat the remaining 1 tablespoon olive oil in a small skillet over high heat until very hot. Add the tomatoes and sauté for 2 minutes, then add the grated garlic and oregano and cook until most of the moisture has evaporated and the tomatoes are crackling.

- Stir the tomatoes into the bean mixture, along with the prosciutto fat. Season with salt and pepper and pour into a 2-quart casserole or baking dish.

- Transfer to the oven and bake for 20 minutes, until the beans are velvety and creamy. If the beans start to look dry, add a splash of water.

- Stir the parsley into the beans, adjust the acidity with white wine vinegar as necessary, and drizzle generously with olive oil. Serve, or keep warm in a low oven until ready to serve.

UKBB (UNITED KINGDOM BAKED BEANS)

Serves 6 to 8

I'm pretty sure that everyone likes baked beans. The English discovered this long-time American staple after the First World War, when meat was hard to come by. Baked beans on toast became the go-to solution for a rib-sticking but economical meal. They're still a hallowed element of an English "full monty breakfast," alongside fried eggs (usually in lard), fried tomatoes, and some back bacon. Like both the British and American versions, my beans are tomato-based, but they are less sweet and thick. They are more savory, with a light smokiness, so that their flavor doesn't dominate other dishes on your plate. Instead, they are a smooth complement.

3 tablespoons vegetable oil

6 slices bacon

½ cup finely diced Spanish onion

6 garlic cloves, finely chopped

1 tablespoon onion powder

1 tablespoon garlic salt

½ teaspoon ground cloves

½ teaspoon ground allspice

Sea or kosher salt and freshly ground black pepper

4 cups cooked white kidney beans or two 15-ounce jars or cans white kidney beans, drained, rinsed if canned

1 cup chicken stock or canned low-sodium broth

3 tablespoons light brown sugar

1 cup ketchup

3 tablespoons white wine vinegar

¼ cup finely chopped fresh flat-leaf parsley

2 tablespoons cold unsalted butter, cut into ½-inch cubes

• Preheat the oven to 225°F.

• Heat the oil in an ovenproof 4-quart pot over medium heat. Add the strips of bacon, the onion, garlic, onion powder, garlic salt, cloves, and allspice, season with salt and pepper, and cook, stirring, until the onion is translucent and the spices are fragrant, 3 to 5 minutes.

• Add the beans and chicken stock, bring to a simmer, and simmer for 10 minutes.

• Stir in the brown sugar, ketchup, and vinegar and bring back to a simmer. Cover, transfer to the oven, and cook for 1 hour. If the beans seem dry, thin slightly with water.

• Set the pot over low heat and stir in the parsley. Swirl in the butter piece by piece until incorporated. Serve, or keep warm in a low oven until ready to serve.

SMOKED-CORN FLAN

Serves 6 to 8

Here we have the very essence of "cornness." In the same way that a glass of fresh-squeezed orange juice gives you the pure flavor of two or three oranges, this custard packs the sweet and savory flavor of half a dozen ears of corn. Setting it in a water bath in the smoker makes for very gentle and even cooking. Cream is, if I may coin a term, flavoristically porous: it picks up smoke in a smoothly sweet way. You will find this flan well suited to fish. Then, if you want a totally contrasting texture, finish the plate with some Crispy Moonshine Onion Rings (page 200).

3 tablespoons unsalted butter,
1 tablespoon softened

2 tablespoons finely chopped shallots

1 tablespoon finely chopped garlic

1 tablespoon chipotle pepper flakes

3 cups corn kernels (from 5 to 6 ears)

Sea or kosher salt and freshly ground black pepper

2 cups heavy cream

2 cups milk

6 large eggs

3 large egg yolks

1 tablespoon fresh thyme leaves

2 tablespoons finely chopped fresh chives

Extra virgin olive oil for drizzling

• Preheat a smoker to 275°F. Butter a 2-quart baking dish with the softened butter.

• Melt the remaining 2 tablespoons butter in a 4-quart pot over medium heat. Add the shallots, garlic, chipotle flakes, and corn and cook, stirring, until the shallots are translucent, 2 to 3 minutes. Season with salt and pepper, cover, and cook until the corn is tender, 4 to 5 minutes. Set aside to cool.

• Whisk together the cream, milk, eggs, and egg yolks in a large bowl. Add the cooled corn mixture, stirring to combine.

• Pour the corn mixture into the buttered baking dish and set the dish in a larger baking pan. Add enough hot water to the baking pan to come halfway up the sides of the baking dish and carefully transfer to the smoker. Cook and smoke for 30 minutes.

- Sprinkle the flan with the thyme, return to the smoker, and smoke for another 15 minutes, or until just set in the center.

- Sprinkle the flan with the chopped chives and drizzle with olive oil. Allow to rest for at least 15 minutes, and up to 1 hour, before serving.

SCRUFFED CARBONARA POTATOES

Serves 8 to 10

Think linguine carbonara, only you can eat it with a spoon. Better yet, think gnocchi, but way easier. Instead of making a traditional potato dough, I trim the potatoes into bite-sized pieces. The sauce provides all the flavor. Just as with pasta carbonara, the serving bowl is preset with the sauce ingredients. The potatoes have enough residual heat to meld them perfectly. And scruffing the potatoes makes for a very clingable surface for the sauce.

3 pounds Yukon Gold potatoes, peeled and cut into 1½-inch pieces

Sea or kosher salt

½ cup extra virgin olive oil, or as needed

4 tablespoons unsalted butter

9 slices bacon, finely chopped

12 garlic cloves, crushed and peeled

2 tablespoons fresh thyme leaves

1 tablespoon fresh rosemary leaves

SAUCE

1 cup extra virgin olive oil

½ cup clarified butter (see Note), melted and still warm

6 large egg yolks, beaten

Sea or kosher salt and freshly ground black pepper

3 to 4 tablespoons freshly squeezed lemon juice

¾ cup freshly grated pecorino romano

¼ cup finely chopped fresh flat-leaf parsley

• Put the potatoes in a 4-quart pot with cold water to cover, add 1 tablespoon salt, and bring to a boil over high heat. Reduce the heat to a gentle simmer and cook until the potatoes are just tender, about 10 minutes.

• Drain the potatoes in a metal colander, reserving ¼ cup of the potato water, and allow the steam to dissipate for 5 minutes. Toss the potatoes in the colander and allow to stand for 5 minutes longer.

• Begin to scruff the potatoes by shaking the colander vigorously from side to side about 15 times. Flip the potatoes and give them another 15 shakes.

• Divide the olive oil and butter between two nonstick skillets that are large enough to hold the potatoes in one layer and heat over medium-high heat until foaming. Add half the potatoes to each pan and cook, without stirring, for 6 minutes. Toss the potatoes and cook for 6 minutes longer, or until the potatoes are golden brown.

- Push the potatoes aside to clear a small space in the center of each pan; if the pan seems dry, add a splash of olive oil and heat until sizzling. Add half the bacon, garlic, thyme, and rosemary to each pan and cook until the herbs are fragrant and the garlic is lightly golden, 2 to 3 minutes. Toss the garlic, bacon, and herbs with the potatoes and cook, stirring occasionally, for 3 to 4 minutes. Transfer to the colander to drain briefly.

- Meanwhile, make the sauce: Mix the oil and warm clarified butter together in a measuring cup or bowl with a spout; set aside.

- Combine the egg yolks and the reserved ¼ cup potato water in a large stainless steel bowl, set over a pot of simmering water, and whisk vigorously until the mixture has doubled in volume and has a velvety texture. Immediately remove from the heat, season with salt and pepper, and add the lemon juice to taste. Gradually whisk in the clarified butter and olive oil.

- Cover the bottom of a warm platter with the egg sauce and arrange the potatoes on top. Sprinkle with the grated pecorino, shower with the chopped parsley, and serve.

NOTE

To clarify butter, start with at least ½ pound unsalted butter. Melt the butter in a heavy saucepan over low heat, without stirring. Skim off the foam that rises to the top. Slowly pour the clear melted butter into a bowl or other container, leaving the milk solids in the bottom of the pan. Clarified butter keeps for weeks in the refrigerator and can also be frozen.

MELTING POTATOES

Serves 6 to 8

Creamy, steaming potatoes have always been a favorite partner for robust grilled meats: potatoes Anna, potatoes au gratin, and scalloped potatoes are dishes I am willing to bet that we have eaten throughout our lives. My contribution to that particular potato pleasure is this dish, which is less calorie rich but as satisfying in every way. I cut the potatoes into rounds and slowly cook them in chicken stock flavored with garlic, thyme, and rosemary. The magic happens when the stock reduces and marries with the starch from the potatoes. It creates a moist, smooth mouthfeel (or, if you will permit a scientific word, viscosity) that has the same sensation as the melted collagen in long-cooked meat like pulled pork, brisket, or leg of lamb. Instead of superstimulating the palate, the potatoes calm it down, which is just what you want to do when serving kick-ass barbecued meat.

2 tablespoons unsalted butter, plus 2 tablespoons cold butter, cut into ½-inch cubes

2 tablespoons extra virgin olive oil, plus more if necessary

5 to 6 russet (baking) potatoes, peeled, cut into ½-inch-thick slices, and edges trimmed to round them

Sea or kosher salt and freshly ground black pepper

15 garlic cloves, crushed and peeled

1 tablespoon fresh thyme leaves

1 tablespoon fresh rosemary leaves

2 cups chicken stock or canned low-sodium broth

1 cup water

2 tablespoons chopped fresh flat-leaf parsley

Juice of ½ lemon, or to taste

• Put 1 tablespoon of the butter and 1 tablespoon of the olive oil in each of two nonstick skillets that are large enough to hold half the potatoes in one layer and heat over medium-high heat until the butter stops crackling. Add half the potatoes to each pan and cook until golden brown on the bottom, about 3 minutes. Flip the potatoes over, season with salt and pepper, and cook until golden brown on the second side, about 3 minutes.

• Push the potatoes aside to clear a small space in the center of each pan; if the pan seems dry, add a splash of olive oil and heat until sizzling. Add half the garlic, thyme, and rosemary to each pan and cook until fragrant, about 2 minutes. Add half the chicken stock and water to each pan and bring to a boil; reduce the heat to a simmer, cover, and cook until the potatoes are just tender, about 15 minutes.

• Remove the lids, raise the heat, and cook until there are just a few tablespoons of liquid remaining in the pans. Remove from the heat and swirl in the cubed butter piece by piece until incorporated, then stir in the parsley. Add a splash of lemon juice, adjust the seasoning, and serve.

POTATO CREAM
WITH LEEKS, CAPERS, AND AVOCADO

Serves 6

If an around-the-world ticket is a little rich for your blood but you find yourself
in New York City, hop on the Number 7 subway to Queens. Every stop puts
you in a different country: Thailand, Spain, Korea, Uruguay, China, Russia,
and more. It's a true melting pot, with lots of different foods melting in lots of
different pots. Over the last few decades, a number of Colombian restaurants
have popped up in Queens to serve that growing immigrant community.
You can find the dish that inspired this recipe at any Colombian restaurant:
ajiaco, a potato and chicken stew with herbs and avocado. My recipe omits the
chicken for a co-star that can go with any number of entrees—say chicken or
lightly smoked cod.

2 tablespoons extra virgin olive oil

1 cup sliced leeks (split the leeks lengthwise first and cut into ¼-inch-thick slices)

½ cup finely chopped Spanish onion

3 garlic cloves, crushed and peeled

Sea or kosher salt and freshly ground black pepper

4 cups ½-inch-dice russet (baking) potatoes

2 cups chicken stock or canned low-sodium broth

2 cups water

1 tablespoon fresh thyme leaves

2 teaspoons dried oregano

¾ cup heavy cream

GARNISHES

¾ cup heavy cream

2 ripe avocados

Generous splash of lemon juice

Sea or kosher salt and freshly ground black pepper

3 tablespoons drained capers

2 tablespoons fresh dill

2 tablespoons chopped fresh chives

2 teaspoons fresh lemon thyme leaves

2 tablespoons extra virgin olive oil

3 lemons, cut in half

- Heat the olive oil in a 4-quart pot over medium-low heat until hot. Add the leeks, onion, and garlic, stir to coat with the oil, and season with a pinch each of salt and pepper. Cover and cook until the onion and garlic are translucent, about 5 minutes.

- Add the potatoes, stock, water, thyme, and oregano, season with salt and pepper, and bring to a boil. Reduce the heat to a simmer and cook until the potatoes are tender, 30 to 40 minutes.

- Add the cream, bring to a simmer, and cook for 10 minutes longer, or until the potatoes are soft.

- Meanwhile, for the garnishes: Whip the cream to semifirm peaks; refrigerate. Halve, peel, and pit the avocados. Cut into ¼-inch-thick slices and toss with the lemon juice and salt and pepper to taste.

- Using an immersion blender, blend the potatoes to a coarse puree; or use a regular blender and pulse just until coarsely pureed, not smooth. The potato cream should have the consistency of a thick soup; if necessary, thin with a little water. Adjust the seasoning if necessary.

- Ladle the potato cream onto a deep platter (if topping with grilled meat) or a serving bowl and swirl in the whipped cream. Scatter the avocado, capers, and herbs over the top, drizzle with the olive oil, and serve with the lemons.

CREAMED SPINACH WITH STEEPED AND SMOKED GARLIC CONFIT

Serves 8 to 12

Creamed spinach is a standby in every steakhouse in America. This version was inspired by the legendary Peter Luger Steak House in Brooklyn's Williamsburg neighborhood. It is the favorite of a lot of New Yorkers, as well as thousands of visitors to the city. By using frozen spinach, you already begin with a soft, almost creamy texture, and you don't have to mask its beautiful green chlorophyll by cooking it forever to soften it. The confited smoked garlic flavors the cream and binds everything together as well as any roux would—and no roux has the deep nutty taste that you get from this garlic confit.

16 garlic cloves, crushed and peeled

1 cup extra virgin olive oil

1 cup finely diced Spanish onion

1 tablespoon sea or kosher salt, or to taste

1 tablespoon garlic powder

1 tablespoon onion powder

1 tablespoon freshly ground white pepper, or to taste

3 cups heavy cream

4 pounds frozen spinach, defrosted, drained, and squeezed dry (2 pounds drained weight)

6 tablespoons unsalted butter, cut into ½-inch cubes and softened

• Preheat a smoker to 275°F.

• Combine the garlic and olive oil in a 4-quart baking dish, put it in the smoker, and cook until the garlic is tender and golden, about 1 hour.

• Preheat the oven to 300°F.

• Transfer the smoked garlic to an 8-quart ovenproof pot, add the onion and salt, and cook over medium-low heat, stirring occasionally, until the onion is translucent.

• Add the garlic powder, onion powder, and white pepper, stirring well. Add the heavy cream, bring to a simmer, and simmer for 10 minutes, stirring occasionally.

• Remove from the heat and stir in the spinach. Transfer to the oven and cook for 45 minutes, or until the spinach is very tender.

• Remove the spinach from the oven and, using an immersion blender, blend until smooth. Add the butter, stirring with a heatproof spatula until it melts. Taste, adjust the seasoning if necessary, and serve.

POLENTA
WITH MASCARPONE AND ROSEMARY

Serves 6 to 8

If there is one thing that always goes with grilled meat, it's thick, creamy polenta made with rich mascarpone. I am indebted to Daniel Boulud for this surefire pleaser, which is one of the most popular dishes we serve at Barbecoa. I put it on a wooden board when the polenta is steaming hot. The mascarpone oozes out of the polenta and then sets up into a thin crust. Rosemary lends a piney note that helps to focus the broad flavors of the cheese and cornmeal.

The wooden board and the rosemary needles remind me of autumn in the Catskills, just across the river from the Culinary Institute of America, where I studied to be a chef. On a crisp October day, this dish has the stick-to-your-ribs heartiness that you long for after a long trudge through the forest when the leaves are falling and the first frost is on the way.

6 cups milk

1 cup heavy cream

3 garlic cloves, crushed and peeled

2 tablespoons fresh rosemary leaves

Sea or kosher salt and freshly ground black pepper

2½ cups instant polenta

3 tablespoons unsalted butter

1 cup freshly grated Parmesan

½ cup mascarpone

2 tablespoons fresh marjoram leaves

Grated zest of 2 lemons

2 tablespoons extra virgin olive oil

• Combine the milk, cream, garlic, rosemary, and salt and pepper to taste in a 4-quart pot and bring just to a boil. Reduce the heat to a lazy simmer and add the polenta in a slow, steady stream, whisking constantly. Cook, stirring frequently, until the polenta is the consistency of thick porridge and smooth.

• Remove from the heat, add the butter, Parmesan, and mascarpone, and whisk in, slowly at first and then increasing the pace, until fully incorporated. Taste and adjust the seasoning. The polenta can be served immediately or kept warm for up to 30 minutes.

• To serve, transfer the polenta to a platter or serving bowl, sprinkle with the marjoram and lemon zest, and drizzle with the olive oil.

CRISPY, FRESH, AND SPRIGHTLY

I think of the ingredients in these co-stars as time-release flavor capsules. By that I mean that you have to chew these crunch-based recipes in order to enjoy the flavor within. As you bite into them, the cadence of chewing changes from simply shearing meat. The crisp and sprightly flavors mix with the barbecued meat, fish, or poultry. The light, refreshing taste and texture add high notes to the overall flavor, extending the pleasure of eating.

62 **Green Apple, Cabbage,
and Caraway Slaw**
Massive crunch, sprightly,
and flavor depth charges
of caraway.

164 **Mango Cilantro Salad**
Sweetness and tanginess
that really snaps the fat in
a pork shoulder or brisket.

166 **Pickled Ramps**
Pungent, sharp, and tangy;
hold their own with deeply
flavored meat.

167 **Radish and Mint Salad**
Crunchy, bitter, peppery,
and cool.

168 **Peach and Nectarine Salad
with Slivered Almonds**
A sweet and tart complement
to rich fish, fowl, or meat.

170 **Lemony Asparagus Shavings
with Goat's-Milk-Curd
Dressing**
Raw asparagus, shaved long
and wafer thin, with a creamy
goat cheese dressing.

172 **Pickled Mixed Vegetables**
Crunchy and tangy; great with
beer and low in calories.

GREEN APPLE, CABBAGE, AND CARAWAY SLAW

Serves 6 to 8

At my first barbecue competition in Des Moines, Iowa, one of the old-timers who was cruising the grounds in a golf cart stopped to chat and then took me under his wing. We started to talk about food, as one deeply interested professional to another.

"I'd love to show you my Walla Walla onions," he said with paternal pride. I'm always glad to taste someone's prize ingredients, and thankful for their sharing.

I think my genuine appreciation of his gesture moved him. With the air of a seasoned veteran offering advice to a newcomer, he said, "If you want to win, think apple."

I gave his advice some serious thought. Champion barbecuers often inject their creations with apple juice or slather them with apple jelly or both. So, as the saying goes, when in Rome . . .

I Microplaned some Granny Smith apples and added them to my board dressing, which was a new way of using an ingredient that the judges knew and liked. The technique has become my secret weapon for waking up barbecue flavors.

This slaw is slightly acidic and tangy from the green apple. It has massive crunch and little flavor capsules of caraway. I love it with the Smoked Pork Shoulder with Lime Coriander Salt (page 40).

6 cups finely shredded green cabbage

2 red bell peppers, cored, seeded, and thinly sliced

2 tablespoons granulated sugar

DRESSING

½ cup mayonnaise

¼ cup sour cream

¼ cup white wine vinegar

2 tablespoons finely chopped Spanish onion

1 tablespoon caraway seeds, toasted in a small skillet and finely ground

Sea or kosher salt and freshly ground black pepper

4 Granny Smith apples, halved, cored, and cut into julienne (skin left on)

2 cups small watercress sprigs

2 tablespoons finely chopped shallots

2 tablespoons thinly sliced (on the bias) red chile pepper

2 tablespoons thinly sliced (on the bias) scallions

½ cup fresh dill leaves

¼ cup chopped fresh flat-leaf parsley

- Combine the cabbage and bell peppers in a large bowl and mix well. Toss with the sugar and allow to macerate for 15 minutes.

- For the dressing, combine all the ingredients in a blender and blend until smooth.

- Add the apples, watercress, shallots, chile pepper, scallions, dill, and parsley to the cabbage and peppers and mix well. Toss with the dressing to coat and serve.

MANGO CILANTRO SALAD

Serves 4 to 6

When I was a young cook, I used to love going down to Chinatown with one of my kitchen comrades, a Vietnamese cook named Si. A favorite destination was a Vietnamese restaurant, Nah Trang, and it's one of my favorites to this day. It is the kind of place where they have Christmas lights up year round, and, somehow, it seems right. The owners would sit us down at a table, and often we were the only people who spoke English, but it didn't matter. We all shared the spirit of great food. They served supercaramelized pork chops, very brown and crunchy and fatty, which called for something that puckered your mouth on a steamy August New York night. Their papaya pickle did the trick.

Taking off from that idea, I decided to combine mango, cilantro, and cucumber—which are all frequently used in Southeast Asian recipes—in a salad. The high acidity of the dressing really snaps the fat in a pork shoulder or brisket.

DRESSING
½ cup freshly squeezed lime juice

2 tablespoons Greek yogurt

¼ cup mild olive oil

Sea or kosher salt and freshly ground black pepper to taste

2 cups julienned unripe mango (about 1 large mango)

1 cup julienned ripe mango

1 cup julienned cucumber

½ cup thinly sliced red onion

¼ cup thinly sliced (on the bias) scallions

½ cup finely chopped fresh cilantro (including some stems)

2 tablespoons thinly slivered (chiffonade) fresh mint leaves

• For the dressing, combine all the ingredients in a small bowl, mixing well.

• Combine the mangoes, cucumber, red onion, scallions, cilantro, and mint in a large bowl, tossing well. Drizzle the dressing over the salad, tossing gently, and serve.

PICKLED RAMPS

Serves 4 to 6

In May, when the dogwoods are in bloom, shad and stripers are running up the Hudson and the Delaware, fiddlehead ferns are the size of quarters, and, if you are lucky, morels are popping up everywhere, you will also find these wild relatives of onions and garlic. I do mean wild! They are supersharp.

I had never tasted pickled ramps until Daniel Boulud gave me some that Gray Kunz had brought to the kitchen from his restaurant, Lespinasse. Even though they are slightly tamed by pickling, they are still pungent, but beautifully acidic and even a little sweet from the brine. This is my version of Gray's pickled ramps. I like it with any collagen-rich, deeply flavored meat.

1 pound ramps, green tops removed

1 cup white wine vinegar

½ cup granulated sugar

1 tablespoon thinly sliced fresh ginger

2 garlic cloves, crushed and peeled

1 red chile pepper, preferably cayenne, seeded and cut lengthwise into 4 strips

1 bay leaf, preferably fresh

1 tablespoon coriander seeds

1½ teaspoons fennel seeds

1 teaspoon black peppercorns

• If necessary, split larger ramps lengthwise in half so they are all about the same thickness. Blanch the ramps in boiling salted water for 10 to 15 seconds, then immediately transfer to a bowl of ice water to cool. Drain and pat lightly dry with paper towels.

• Put the ramps in a canning jar that holds them loosely, and set aside.

• Combine the vinegar, sugar, ginger, garlic, chile pepper, bay leaf, coriander seeds, fennel seeds, and peppercorns in a medium saucepan and bring to a simmer, stirring to dissolve the sugar.

• Pour the brine over the ramps and seal the jar. Allow to cool, then refrigerate for at least 12 hours before serving. The ramps will keep for at least 5 days in the refrigerator.

RADISH AND MINT SALAD

Serves 6 to 8

In my childhood, I didn't have a high opinion of radishes. If I considered them at all, I thought of them as the red things served alongside the celery, carrots, and olives in ice-filled bowls at Italian restaurants on Long Island. Almost tasteless vegetables to munch and crunch on while you waited for your lasagna or eggplant parmigiano.

Years later, I came to regard Alice Waters's *Vegetables* as a bible, so I took it to heart when she said that you need to rethink your prejudices. I decided to give radishes another shot. It was worth it. When I worked in France, I learned to love braised radishes. The French also serve raw radishes with coarse salt and fresh creamery butter, or sometimes anchovy butter.

Radishes are crunchy, bitter, peppery, and cool. Adding mint makes them grassy and even cooler.

VINAIGRETTE

1 tablespoon freshly squeezed lemon juice

Sea or kosher salt and freshly ground black pepper

2 tablespoons mild olive oil

¼ cup thinly sliced (on the bias) scallions

2 tablespoons thinly sliced shallots

1 tablespoon thinly sliced red chile pepper

1 cup julienned peeled daikon radish

1 cup quartered breakfast radishes

1 cup thinly sliced red radishes

1 cup arugula leaves

1 cup julienned endive

3 tablespoons torn fresh mint leaves

• For the vinaigrette, whisk together the lemon juice and salt and pepper to taste in a small bowl, then whisk in the olive oil. Whisk in the scallions, shallots, and chile pepper.

• Toss all the radishes together in a medium bowl. Add the arugula, endive, and mint, tossing gently. Toss with just enough vinaigrette to coat and serve.

PEACH AND NECTARINE SALAD WITH SLIVERED ALMONDS

Serves 4 to 6

I was once hired to do some consulting for the Peach, Plum, and Nectarine Board in California. It didn't require a lot of convincing. I am mad about stone fruit. I think all of us can remember that perfect one that we had on a summer's day. For me, it was a peach. I was twenty-two years old and attending the Culinary Institute of America when I stopped at a Hudson Valley farm stand whose display beckoned to me. The deep green fields, the blue and sunlit ribbon of the Hudson, and the ancient Catskill Mountains make this one of the most beautiful landscapes on earth.

That memorable peach was of such ripe juiciness that I tried, as one does, to eat it by leaning over it so most of me was out of squirt-and-drip range. Somehow, this strategy never completely works and sweet, ripe juicy peaches and nectarines will always find a way to drip down your chin no matter what you do.

This salad makes for a sweet, nicely acidic complement to fattier fish such as the underappreciated bluefish, which run off the East Coast just about the time that peaches and nectarines are happening. I throw in slivered almonds for some contrasting bitterness and crunch so that it's not simply soft fruit. Try this with grilled sausages as well, or any cut of pork or lamb.

2 tablespoons granulated sugar

4 peaches, halved and pitted

1 tablespoon unsalted butter

4 nectarines, halved, pitted, and cut into ⅛-inch-thick slivers

2 tablespoons finely chopped red onion

2 cups tender dandelion greens or arugula leaves

½ cup chopped fresh cilantro

2 tablespoons freshly squeezed lime juice

1 tablespoon mild olive oil

Sea or kosher salt and freshly ground black pepper

Aged balsamic vinegar for drizzling

Extra virgin olive oil for drizzling

¼ cup toasted slivered almonds

- Spread the sugar on a plate and coat the cut sides of the peaches with the sugar.

- Heat a flat cast-iron griddle or large cast-iron skillet over medium-high heat until hot. Add the butter and let it melt. Add the peaches, cut side down, and cook until well caramelized on the cut surfaces, 4 to 5 minutes. Transfer to a plate.

- Combine the nectarines, red onion, dandelion greens, and cilantro in a medium bowl. Add the lime juice, mild olive oil, and salt and pepper to taste and toss gently.

- Mound the nectarine salad in the center of a platter and arrange the caramelized peaches, cut side up, around it. Drizzle with balsamic vinegar and extra virgin olive oil, sprinkle with the toasted almonds, and serve.

LEMONY ASPARAGUS SHAVINGS WITH GOAT'S-MILK-CURD DRESSING

Serves 4 to 6

I will never forget a demo that Mario Batali gave where he shaved raw asparagus with a potato peeler. The resultant green strands were like asparagus fettuccine—long and wafer-thin. It was nothing short of a revelation when I tasted them after he'd dressed the shavings with lemon juice: the cell walls of the raw asparagus were broken, I realized, and soaked up dressing beautifully, slightly tenderizing the crisp asparagus but still preserving some of their pleasing snap. Creamy goat cheese provided the perfect textural counterpoint and also had enough acidity to unify the dish.

My version calls for fresh thyme and lemon zest, and I always use goat's-milk curds. Regular goat cheese is also fine, but if you are near a farmers' market that sells goat cheese, ask for the curds. They stay pristinely white in this salad, which never fails to impress guests—not to mention your own palate.

1 pound pencil asparagus, bottom ¼ inch of stalks cut off

15 to 20 thick asparagus spears, bottom ¼ inch of stalks cut off

DRESSING

1 cup (8 ounces) goat's-milk curds or 8 ounces fresh goat cheese

2 cups goat's milk or regular milk, or to taste

3 tablespoons mild olive oil

2 teaspoons fresh thyme leaves

Sea or kosher salt and freshly ground black pepper

3 tablespoons finely chopped shallots

¼ cup freshly squeezed lemon juice

¼ cup extra virgin olive oil

Sea or kosher salt and freshly ground black pepper

2 tablespoons finely chopped fresh chives

Grated zest of 2 lemons

- Blanch the pencil asparagus in a large pot of boiling salted water for 1 minute. Immediately transfer to a bowl of ice water to cool, then remove from the ice water and drain on paper towels. Put in a medium bowl and set aside.

- Using a vegetable peeler, shave the thick asparagus into ribbons. Transfer to another medium bowl.

- For the dressing, put the goat's-milk curds in a large bowl and gently whisk in the milk. Whisk in the olive oil, thyme, and salt and pepper to taste. Add more milk if needed to loosen the consistency; it should be similar to pancake batter.

- Toss the blanched asparagus with half the shallots, lemon juice, and olive oil and season with salt and pepper to taste. Toss the shaved asparagus with the remaining shallots, lemon juice, and olive oil and season with salt and pepper.

- Spoon the dressing onto individual plates, spreading it evenly. Arrange the asparagus stalks on top, followed by the asparagus shavings. Sprinkle with the chives and lemon zest and serve.

PICKLED MIXED VEGETABLES

Serves 4 to 6

Crudites and dip are a time-honored way to give guests something to eat while you are waiting for the barbecue—and great with beer. The flavors in the pickling brine for these vegetables add tang, spiced aromatic notes, and peppery heat. So simple, yet so powerful.

2 cups white wine vinegar

2 cups water

½ cup granulated sugar

3 garlic cloves, crushed and peeled

8 fresh thyme branches

¼ cup small fresh cilantro sprigs

1 tablespoon coriander seeds

1 teaspoon black peppercorns

1 cup 3-inch-long carrot batons (¼ inch thick)

1 cup halved red radishes

1 cup 1-inch cauliflower florets

2 mild red chile peppers, split and seeds removed

1 cup quartered red onions (leave enough of the root ends to keep the onion quarters intact)

½ cup ½-inch-wide red bell pepper strips

- Combine all the ingredients in a large stainless steel or other nonreactive saucepan and bring to a simmer over medium heat. Cover and cook for 5 minutes. Remove from the heat and allow to cool.

- Refrigerate the vegetables for at least 24 hours before serving; they will keep for 2 to 3 days, tightly covered, in the refrigerator.

Crispy, sprightly co-stars add bright fresh flavors to complement deep, rich meats.

LEAVES, LETTUCES, AND GREENS

Leafy vegetables are filling but not fattening. They require chewing time, so they slow your rhythm. They carry acid beautifully, which makes your mouth water. This combination of salivating plus acid flavor cuts through the rich and mouth-coating feel of collagen in properly barbecued meat.

Some of the best co-star greens are bitter greens. I have often wondered why we would want to eat anything bitter. On their own, bitter things are not pleasurable. But with meat, especially fatty meat, the bitterness helps to cut through the crescendo of flavor that would eventually overwhelm your palate. Even if I served you the best, smokiest, most tender ribs in the whole city of Memphis, Tennessee, they would get boring if not complemented by a contrasting taste.

So, for the relief of temporary culinary boredom, I offer the following recipes.

178 **Charred Radicchio
with Sweet-and-Sticky
Balsamic and Bacon**
Bitter yet sweet; a great
counterpoint to rich
main courses.

182 **Fleur's Butter Lettuce
Salad with Pommery
Mustard Dressing**
An homage to my
wife, her dad, and an
underappreciated green.

184 **Watercress with Pickled
Garlic and Smoked Anchovies**
The names of the ingredients
pretty much tell the tale: flavor,
flavor, and more flavor.

186 **Belgian Endive Salad
with Burnt Oranges,
Marjoram Dressing,
and Pomegranate Seeds**
Bitter, fruity, herbal, juicy,
and crunchy.

188 **Arugula Salad with Lemon,
Extra Virgin Olive Oil,
and Parmesan Shavings**
Nothing could be simpler to
make. Deep flavor.

190 **Baby Beet Greens and
Mâche with Balsamic
and Shaved Pecorino**
Sweet, earthy, sharp, and
tangy. Great all year.

192 **Warm Crunchy Broccolini
with Prosciutto and
Scruffed Croutons**
A fresh green salad with mucho
flavor, mucho crunch.

CHARRED RADICCHIO WITH SWEET-AND-STICKY BALSAMIC AND BACON

Serves 8 to 10

When I am sitting in a business meeting, I often daydream about food, as I was on the day when we had a meeting in Jamie Oliver's conference room. On the wall, there was a stunning, poetic picture of radicchio wrapped in bacon, just about to go into the oven. I thought about how it would taste. Actually, I think the impression was so strong that I truly tasted it. And then, as people who think about food tend to do, I thought about what I might do with radicchio.

I visualized grilling its deep-red leaves to a bitter char that would match the char on a piece of grilled meat. The soft grilled leaves would respond well to the sticky-sweet acidity of good balsamic vinegar. It fills the mouth with bitter sweetness, a well-matched foil to Double-Butterflied Leg of Lamb (page 50) or Roasted Rib Stack with Worcestershire Salt (page 42). And the bacon makes it all better, because that's the great culinary virtue of smoky, fatty cured pork.

Here is that daydream on a plate.

VINAIGRETTE
2 tablespoons sherry vinegar

2 tablespoons finely chopped shallots

1 teaspoon red pepper flakes

1 teaspoon garlic paste (1 to 2 cloves mashed with a pinch of salt)

Pinch each of sea or kosher salt and freshly ground black pepper

2 tablespoons extra virgin olive oil

1 teaspoon dried oregano

1 teaspoon fresh thyme leaves

¼ cup chopped fresh flat-leaf parsley

4 to 5 heads radicchio, quartered and core trimmed

16 to 20 slices bacon

2 tablespoons aged balsamic vinegar

¼ cup extra virgin olive oil

2 tablespoons chopped fresh chives

• Preheat the grill to medium-low.

• For the vinaigrette, whisk all the ingredients together in a small bowl.

• Put the radicchio in a large bowl and drizzle with just enough vinaigrette to coat lightly, tossing gently.

• Lay a slice of bacon on a work surface and wrap a radicchio quarter tightly in the bacon, starting from the bottom end and continuing to just shy of ¼ inch from the top. Repeat with the remaining bacon and radicchio.

• Put the radicchio quarters on the oiled clean grill grate and cook until crispy and golden on the first side, about 2 minutes. Turn and cook until crisp and golden on the second side, about 2 minutes, then turn and cook until crisp and golden on the third side.

• Transfer the radicchio to a platter. Drizzle with the balsamic vinegar and olive oil, sprinkle with the chopped chives, and serve.

Radicchio leaves aren't hydrated, unlike most other lettuces. As a result, radicchio is built to grill: it doesn't leach out water during cooking or wilt too much and it's tong-friendly.

FLEUR'S BUTTER LETTUCE SALAD WITH POMMERY MUSTARD DRESSING

Serves 8 to 10

This salad was named after my wife, Fleur. She always makes a salad with soft butter lettuce, as it is often called in our new hometown of London. But I still like its more American name, Bibb lettuce. It is said to have been first grown in Kentucky, where the limestone soil accounts for the best bourbon-making water. The Pommery mustard is full of tiny mustard seeds that pop when you chew them, like caviar or tapioca or champagne grapes.

Serve with roast chicken or stronger-tasting (oily) fish, such as salmon, mackerel, or bluefish.

VINAIGRETTE
2 tablespoons Pommery mustard

¼ cup champagne vinegar

2 tablespoons finely chopped shallots

Sea or kosher salt and freshly ground black pepper to taste

¼ cup mild extra virgin olive oil

2 to 3 medium vine-ripened or heirloom tomatoes, thinly sliced

1 teaspoon sea or kosher salt

1 teaspoon freshly ground black pepper

2 tablespoons finely chopped fresh chives

2 heads butter lettuce, leaves separated

2 tablespoons fresh dill leaves

• For the vinaigrette, whisk all the ingredients together in a small bowl.

• Arrange the tomatoes on a large rimmed plate and season with the salt and pepper. Sprinkle with the chives. Pour the vinaigrette over the tomatoes and let macerate for 10 minutes.

• Arrange the tomatoes on a large platter, leaving the vinaigrette on the plate.

• Put the lettuce and dill in a large bowl and drizzle with the vinaigrette, tossing gently to coat. Arrange the lettuce on top of the tomatoes and serve.

WATERCRESS WITH PICKLED GARLIC AND SMOKED ANCHOVIES

Serves 8 to 10

The names of the ingredients pretty much tell the tale: this recipe screams flavor. It started with a visit to Brindisa, an amazing Spanish delicacy store in London's Borough Market. Fish, cheese, sausages, hams, the world's best coffee, freshly made wraps of griddled shrimp, and crunchy vegetables—it is a food lover's heaven.

One of my chefs and I found ourselves in Brindisa a few months ago and we started to nosh on their pickled garlic. I don't know quite how they do it, but somewhere in the process, the brine takes away all the sharpness of the garlic. You have to try it for yourself (available in some Spanish and Middle Eastern markets). Once it's been tamed by the brine, you can eat garlic to your heart's content and still have a social life with those who don't worship this divine bulb.

Another of the Brindisa items I have grown fond of is smoked anchovies. One day, a little voice from inside the anchovy tin said, "Mix me with that garlic and some watercress." Or maybe it was just my culinary imagination.

Note to self: bring these along to a Korean restaurant the next time I have short ribs grilled tableside. I think it will be a much more satisfying experience than eating the raw garlic I have with this dish whenever I go to Koreatown.

Look for pickled garlic cloves and smoked anchovies at Spanish markets, at gourmet shops, or online (see Sources, page 256).

VINAIGRETTE
Juice of 1 lemon

1 teaspoon sherry vinegar

1 tablespoon finely chopped shallot

2 tablespoons extra virgin olive oil

Sea or kosher salt and freshly ground black pepper

¼ cup halved pickled garlic cloves

16 to 20 smoked anchovy fillets, cut lengthwise into 3 strips each (or substitute anchovies packed in olive oil)

¼ cup finely diced jarred piquillo peppers

5 to 6 cups watercress sprigs

¼ cup fresh flat-leaf parsley leaves

1 tablespoon fresh marjoram leaves

- For the vinaigrette, whisk all the ingredients together in a small bowl.

- Transfer 2 tablespoons of the vinaigrette to a large bowl and add the pickled garlic, anchovies, and diced peppers, tossing to coat. Add the watercress and herbs and toss lightly, adding just enough vinaigrette to coat. Serve.

BELGIAN ENDIVE SALAD WITH BURNT ORANGES, MARJORAM DRESSING, AND POMEGRANATE SEEDS

Serves 8 to 10

When oranges are halved and cooked on a griddle, or *plancha*, the result is burnt (but not to the point of bitter carbonization) on the cooked side and then progressively less cooked as you eat your way through them. It makes for a very interesting taste narrative. Pete explored burnt oranges with the Argentinean master chef Francis Mallmann in a great dessert in their book *Seven Fires*. They work just as well in a savory course.

Endives add watery crunch. The crowning touch is marjoram, an herb that I was not truly familiar with until I came to England. We just don't use it that much in the United States. It's like a pungent cross between oregano and rosemary, only more floral, and marjoram seems to retain its highly flavorful oils more than oregano or rosemary. A food scientist would say the oils don't volatilize as readily, but you don't need science to know and appreciate the flavor. It works particularly well with bitter greens.

¼ cup granulated sugar

4 to 5 oranges, peel and all white pith removed, cut in half

¼ cup fresh marjoram leaves

VINAIGRETTE

3 tablespoons champagne vinegar

1 tablespoon finely chopped shallot

1 tablespoon crème fraîche or Greek yogurt

Sea or kosher salt and freshly ground black pepper to taste

3 tablespoons mild extra virgin olive oil

6 to 8 Belgian endives, cut lengthwise in half, cored, and cut on the bias into 1-inch-wide pieces

2 tablespoons ½-inch batons fresh chives

Seeds from 2 pomegranates

- Spread the sugar on a large plate and put the oranges cut side down on the sugar.

- Heat a large cast-iron pan over high heat until it just starts to smoke. Pierce an orange half with a fork and transfer to the hot pan, sugar side down; repeat with the remaining oranges. Cook until the cut surfaces of the oranges are deeply caramelized, about 2 minutes. Transfer the oranges, cut side up, to a platter and sprinkle with the marjoram. Set aside.

- For the vinaigrette, whisk all the ingredients together in a small bowl.

- Put the endive in a large bowl and toss with just enough vinaigrette to coat lightly. Transfer to a platter, arrange the caramelized oranges around the endive, sprinkle with the chive batons and pomegranate seeds, and serve.

ARUGULA SALAD
WITH LEMON, EXTRA VIRGIN OLIVE OIL,
AND PARMESAN SHAVINGS

Serves 8 to 10

There may be no simpler recipe in this book, but its clarity of flavor and texture plays consummate counterpoint to the densely layered notes of meat, herbs, salt, and smoke. Try it with High-Low Boneless Rib Eye (page 62) or Thick Pork Chops, Guaranteed Juicy (page 76). The strong mouth-puckering acidity of cut-up lemon segments breaks the mouth-coating effect of fat like a slap of bay rum on your face after a shave. Baby or young arugula is the way to go. The arugula should be slightly bitter to encourage the tasting process to come to a halt, which can then start anew with the next bite, but superbitter, mature arugula is unpleasant. For a seasonal change, substitute dandelion greens for the arugula, as pictured opposite.

VINAIGRETTE

Juice of 2 lemons

1 tablespoon white wine vinegar

¼ teaspoon granulated sugar

Sea or kosher salt and freshly ground black pepper to taste

¼ cup extra virgin olive oil

2 lemons

10 cups arugula leaves

¼ cup fresh flat-leaf parsley leaves

¼ cup fresh dill leaves

¼ cup ½-inch batons fresh chives

¼ cup Parmesan shavings (use a vegetable peeler)

• For the vinaigrette, whisk all the ingredients together in a small bowl. Set aside.

• Using a sharp serrated or other knife, cut off the top and bottom of each lemon to expose the flesh. Stand each lemon up on the cutting board and carefully cut away the skin and bitter white pith in strips, working from top to bottom and following the natural curve of the fruit. Trim away any remaining pith.

• To remove the lemon segments (suprêmes), work over a bowl and cut down along the membranes on either side of each section to release it, letting the sections drop into the bowl as you go. Cut each segment crosswise in half.

• Combine the arugula, parsley, and dill in a large salad bowl. Add the lemon segments, then toss gently with just enough vinaigrette to coat. Scatter the chive batons and Parmesan shavings over the top and serve.

BABY BEET GREENS AND MÂCHE WITH BALSAMIC AND SHAVED PECORINO

Serves 8 to 10

People often serve beets with balsamic, but for something different and more leafy/crunchy, I use tender young beet greens. I have no problem with hydroponically grown ones, which are apt to be fresher in winter than greens grown in sunlight and shipped thousands of miles. You definitely get the savory taste of beets from their greens. Aged balsamic vinegar adds acid as it contributes beetroot color and some sweetness. The pecorino provides umami, adding power to the flavor so that this salad can be served with any barbecued meat or chicken.

VINAIGRETTE

¼ cup champagne vinegar

1 teaspoon Dijon mustard

1 tablespoon finely chopped shallot

Sea or kosher salt and freshly ground black pepper to taste

½ cup mild extra virgin olive oil

5 cups baby beet greens

5 cups mâche

1 cup quartered breakfast radishes

½ cup thinly sliced red onion (cut the onion in half before slicing)

2 tablespoons aged balsamic vinegar

¼ cup aged pecorino shavings (use a vegetable peeler)

• For the vinaigrette, whisk all the ingredients together in a small bowl.

• Combine the beet greens, mâche, radishes, and red onion in a large salad bowl and toss with just enough vinaigrette to coat. Drizzle with the balsamic, scatter the pecorino shavings over the top, and serve.

WARM CRUNCHY BROCCOLINI WITH PROSCIUTTO AND SCRUFFED CROUTONS

Serves 4 to 6

Along about the time that I have had enough of winter, and even the best caramelized root vegetables and braised cabbage have ceased to hold any allure (at least until next winter), the first greens of spring appear in the market. Broccolini arrives like a bright green promise of the coming season's fresh bounty. It can become strong tasting as the season wears on, but at this time of year it has just the right amount of slight bitterness and doesn't require long cooking. A quick blanching does the trick but leaves it fresh and crunchy. Finish with roughly cut croutons (see The Art of Scruffing, page 8) and strips of prosciutto for a fresh salad packed with flavor. Serve with anything grilled— or add some cheese and charcuterie for a light stand-alone meal.

VINAIGRETTE

2 tablespoons finely chopped shallots

1 teaspoon Colman's dry mustard

½ teaspoon granulated sugar

Juice of 2 lemons

2 tablespoons white wine vinegar

1 tablespoon finely chopped red chile pepper, such as cayenne

½ teaspoon red pepper flakes, soaked in 1 tablespoon boiling water (to bring out the flavor)

Sea or kosher salt and freshly ground black pepper to taste

¾ cup extra virgin olive oil

4 cups 1-inch pieces broccolini (florets and stems)

CROUTONS

3 tablespoons unsalted butter

3 tablespoons extra virgin olive oil

2 cups torn rustic Italian bread (approximately ½-inch pieces)

5 garlic cloves, crushed and peeled

2 tablespoons fresh rosemary leaves

4 ounces thinly sliced (⅛-inch-thick) prosciutto, cut into ⅛-inch-wide strips

1 teaspoon garlic salt

1 teaspoon freshly ground black pepper

Sea or kosher salt and freshly ground black pepper

Extra virgin olive oil for drizzling

2 lemons, cut in half

- For the vinaigrette, whisk all the ingredients together in a small bowl. Set aside.

- Blanch the broccolini in a large pot of boiling salted water for 3 minutes. Drain and immediately transfer to a bowl of ice water to cool. Remove from the ice water and drain on paper towels.

- For the croutons, combine the butter and olive oil in a skillet large enough to hold the pieces of bread in a single layer and heat until crackling. Add the bread, garlic, and rosemary, stirring to coat the bread, and cook, stirring and shaking the pan, until the croutons are golden brown. Remove from the heat, add the prosciutto, tossing to mix, and season with the garlic salt and pepper. Transfer to a plate and allow to cool.

- To serve, toss the broccolini with the vinaigrette and adjust the seasoning with salt and pepper if necessary. Arrange on a platter and scatter the croutons over the top. Drizzle with a little olive oil and garnish the platter with the lemon halves.

CRISPY BITS

Why do we love the combination of crispy, salty, and hot? I believe it has something to do with the fact that humans have always been meat eaters. It's a sure bet that there were no vegan Neanderthals. The fact of the matter is, whenever you put meat on a fire, you get a hot, crispy crust. As for the salty, we crave it because it is necessary for our survival. When you put some salt on grilled meat, it's the best!

"But french-fried potatoes and onion rings aren't meat!" you might say. Think about it. You can imagine barbecue without coleslaw, or baked beans, or macaroni and cheese. But no french fries, or crispy fried anything? Does not compute.

198 **Duck-Fat Fries**
The crispiest, most savory
fries you've ever had.

199 **Chicken Skin Cooked and
Crisped Under a Brick**
Salty, herby, garlicky, and
crisp as a potato chip, it's the
most fun part of the chicken,
done to perfection.

200 **Crispy Moonshine
Onion Rings**
Clear booze and batter
are the secret to succulent,
crisp onion rings, with a
flavor jolt of whiskey.

202 **Supercrisp Pork Rinds**
By boiling, then frying, these
are the crispiest, cracklingest
pork rinds I have ever tasted.

204 **Fried Shallot Loaf**
Good with everything . . .
or all by itself.

DUCK-FAT FRIES

Serves 6 to 8

I've been in restaurant kitchens all of my working life, so it's fair to say if you can fry with it, I've probably tried it. Olive oil, canola, butter, lard, and all of the industrial superhydrogenated goo that has received justifiably bad press in recent years because it is unhealthful. To my palate, all these fats also produce fries that taste blah.

After working with every frying medium, I now use duck fat for my french-fried potatoes. Having served thousands of orders of duck-fat fries, I can tell you that it's a rare day at my restaurant when a customer doesn't eat them all. That's the best test I know for a successful recipe.

3 quarts duck fat	2 tablespoons olive oil
2½ pounds russet (baking) potatoes (8 medium to large potatoes)	2 tablespoons finely chopped fresh flat-leaf parsley
2 garlic cloves, grated (use a Microplane)	1 tablespoon Wine Vinegar Salt (page 251)

• Heat the duck fat to 325°F in a large pot. Meanwhile, cut the unpeeled potatoes into ¼-inch-thick french fries. Transfer to a colander and rinse under cold water until the water runs clear. Drain, then pat lightly dry with paper towels.

• A handful at a time, add the potatoes to the hot fat and cook for 3 minutes to blanch them. Remove with a spider or slotted spoon, transfer to a baking sheet, and allow to cool. Set the pot of oil aside until just before serving time. (You can cook the potatoes to this point up to 3 hours ahead.)

• When ready to serve, heat the duck fat to 325°F again. Combine the garlic and olive oil in a small cup.

• Working in batches, add the potatoes to the hot fat, without crowding the pot, and fry until golden brown, 3 to 4 minutes. Transfer to a large stainless steel bowl. Scatter the parsley, garlic oil, and salt over the hot fries, tossing to distribute the seasonings evenly, and serve.

CHICKEN SKIN COOKED AND CRISPED UNDER A BRICK

Serves 6 to 8

Among the handful of universal truths in eating, I never met anyone who didn't like crisped chicken skin. If you give a kid a choice between chicken meat and chicken skin, you know they're going to choose the skin. This recipe, where the skin is hydrated with water, garlic, and herbs and then crisped under a brick, is unbelievably flavorful as well as enjoyably crisp.

2 pounds chicken skin

1 tablespoon Four Seasons Blend (page 7)

1 teaspoon garlic salt

1 teaspoon freshly ground black pepper

1 tablespoon finely chopped fresh flat-leaf parsley

A clean brick, wrapped in foil

• Preheat the oven to 350°F.

• Season the chicken skin with the seasoning blend. Line a baking sheet with a nonstick baking mat or parchment paper and spread the chicken skin on it. Cover with another baking mat or sheet of parchment, set another baking sheet on top, and put the brick on top of the baking sheet to weight it down.

• Put the chicken skin in the oven and cook for 20 minutes. Remove from the oven, being mindful of the rendered fat, remove the brick and the top baking sheet and baking mat, and carefully pour off the fat.

• Lightly dab the skin with a paper towel and put the baking mat, baking sheet, and brick back on top. Continue to cook, checking after 15 minutes and then every 5 minutes thereafter, until the skin is golden brown and crispy, about 40 minutes in all.

• Using tongs, transfer the hot skin to a large bowl and toss with the garlic salt, pepper, and parsley, then immediately transfer to a wire cooling rack. Allow to cool and crisp for 5 minutes, and serve.

CRISPY MOONSHINE ONION RINGS

Serves 6 to 8

It has been known for some time that using vodka—which evaporates quickly—or club soda instead of water makes for less watery batter. David Chang is one of many modern chefs who has used vodka this way. It got me thinking: if vodka works, how about my own custom-made moonshine?

8 cups peanut oil

3 large Spanish onions, cut into ½-inch-thick slices and separated into rings

1 cup milk

2 cups all-purpose flour

2 teaspoons sea or kosher salt, plus more for sprinkling

2 teaspoons freshly ground black pepper

BATTER

4 large egg whites

1 cup Original Moonshine clear corn whiskey or vodka

2 cups cornstarch

2 teaspoons sea or kosher salt

2 teaspoons freshly ground black pepper

2 teaspoons cayenne pepper

About 4 cups panko crumbs

• Heat the oil to 350°F in an 8-quart pot. Meanwhile, put the onions in a large bowl and pour the milk over them to moisten them; drain.

• Put the flour in a large sealable plastic bag, add the salt and pepper, and shake to mix. Working in batches, add the drained onion slices to the flour, seal the bag, and shake vigorously to coat the slices, then spread on a baking sheet.

• For the batter, whip the egg whites to soft peaks in a large bowl. Fold in the moonshine. Sift the cornstarch, salt, black pepper, and cayenne over the egg whites and fold in gently.

• Spread the panko crumbs evenly on a baking sheet. Line another baking sheet with paper towels.

• Working in batches, add the onion rings to the batter, then, one at a time, toss onto the panko crumbs and flip over to coat with crumbs; repeat until you have filled the baking sheet with a generously spaced layer of onions.

• One by one, drop the coated onions into the hot oil, without crowding, and cook until golden brown, 3 to 4 minutes. Remove with a spider or slotted spoon, transfer to the lined baking sheet to drain briefly, and sprinkle with salt, then transfer to a mesh cooling rack (this will prevent the onion rings from becoming soggy). Repeat with the remaining onion rings and serve.

SUPERCRISP PORK RINDS

Serves 8 to 10

Pork rinds have finally begun to achieve their rightful place in American food culture. Once they were a Southern or Mexican treat, but now everybody loves them. The trick is boiling, baking, and finally frying to supercrispiness.

5 pounds pork skin with rind (4 sheets approximately 12 by 12 inches and ¼ inch thick)

2 tablespoons sea or kosher salt

1 lemon, cut in half

3 quarts vegetable oil

Four Seasons Blend (page 7), for sprinkling

- Put the pork skin in a large pot, add the salt and enough water to cover generously. Squeeze each lemon half into the pot and then drop the halves into the water. Bring to a boil over high heat. Reduce to a low boil and cook until the skin is extremely tender, just shy of falling apart, about 3 hours; replenish the water as necessary.

- Line a large baking dish with plastic wrap and layer the pork skin in the dish (if it falls apart a bit, just fit it back together again like patchwork). Cover the dish with plastic wrap, place a baking pan that just fits inside the dish on top, and weight with a couple of heavy cans or a brick. Refrigerate for at least 6 hours; the layered skin should be very firm and solid.

- Heat the oil to 350°F in a large pot. Meanwhile, remove the weights and top layer of plastic wrap from the baking dish, turn the pork skin out onto a cutting board, and peel off the remaining plastic wrap. Using a meat fork to anchor the skin, cut it into ¼-inch-wide strips with a serrated knife.

- Working in batches, add the pork skin to the hot oil (taking care to protect yourself from the popping skin—use a spatter shield if you have one) and fry for 10 to 12 minutes, until crisp and golden brown. (The pork skin will pop and sizzle at first and then stop crackling—it may seem as if nothing is happening, but it will become tender and crispy in the silent oil.) Remove with a spider or slotted spoon and immediately sprinkle with the seasoning blend. Serve hot, or keep warm in a low oven until ready to serve; or allow to cool and serve at room temperature.

FRIED SHALLOT LOAF

Serves 8 to 10

While there are a million recipes that start out with the instruction "chop the shallots and sauté until golden," there are too few that focus on this relative of garlic and onions. The oniony flavor and aroma of shallots seems to caress every iota of flavor in grilled food, especially meat. They bring out sweetness and savoriness simultaneously. Batter-fried crispness punches it all home.

Vegetable oil for deep-frying

5 cups all-purpose flour

1 tablespoon garlic salt

2½ pounds shallots (about 20 shallots), sliced ⅛ inch thick and separated into rings

1 quart milk

3 large eggs, lightly beaten

Sea or kosher salt

• Preheat the oil to 350°F in a deep fryer (see Note). Meanwhile, combine the flour and garlic salt in a large bowl and mix well. Put the shallots in a medium bowl and pour the milk and eggs over them, stirring to combine.

• Gently lift out the shallot rings a handful at a time, with some of the milk and egg clinging to them, and toss with the seasoned flour; the shallots will be a bit sticky and clumpy. Put the fryer basket into the fryer, drop in all the floured shallots in an even layer, and immediately put a second fryer basket on top to compress the shallots and submerge them in the oil. Fry until golden brown, 3 to 4 minutes. Carefully remove the shallots from the basket and drain briefly on paper towels, then transfer to a rack and season with salt. Serve immediately.

NOTE

If you don't have a deep fryer and two fryer baskets, heat 3 inches of oil in a large, deep pot and cook the shallots in batches, adding them in clumps to the hot oil to make free-form "cakes," or fritters.

Part IV

FINISHING

SPACKLES

I often describe these recipes as something you spackle onto a forkful of something else, and in fact, I call some of them "spackles." By that I mean they are not what you would think of as a side dish, but neither do they qualify as typical condiments. They are textural, highly flavored, often highly reduced and concentrated ingredients that you just dip into or dab onto a forkful of barbecue. These spackles are a finishing touch, a powerful uppercut that jolts the senses.

The idea of spackling on flavors came from an understanding of what it takes to win a barbecue competition. I realized that the judges were eating only a bite each before giving their verdict. So I knew I had to punch them hard to make my entries stand out. I also realized that smoke, although wonderful, can numb the palate. Simply repeating a critical element that everyone else used ran the risk of not being special.

My fork finishers are all about big flavors to jar and wake up your taste buds. They also give your mouth so much to "think" about that you slow down, prolonging the pleasure. They are punctuation marks that make food exciting. Acid is a key part of these spackles. Not only does it kick-start salivation, it has a fat-breaking quality that strips/degreases the tongue a bit. Great smoky barbecued meat is a potentially overwhelming component that will eventually lose its ability to please without some acid to break up its hold on your palate. With these fork finishers, vinegar, or lemon juice, or wine rides in to the rescue.

Some of these finishers will be familiar to you in their less concentrated forms as a side dish. For example, the ingredients in the caponata finisher (page 224) are not much different from what goes into the classic dish—but I put the ingredients on a parchment-lined pan and dry them in a dehydrator or low oven so that the flavor is superconcentrated. Think about the difference between the taste of ketchup and that of a slice of tomato. They start from the same place, but the intensity of flavor is vastly different.

I also like to include raw or less-cooked versions of some of the ingredients, contrasting caramelized and crunchy.

212   Red Pepper Spackle

214   Mango Spackle

216   Cranberry Spackle

218   Tomato Spackle

220   Artichoke Spackle

222   Hatch Chile Spackle

224   Concentrated Caponata

RED PEPPER SPACKLE

Makes 3 cups

Caramelizing and concentrating the flavor of the garlic and onion creates a smooth, velvety underscoring flavor base that bridges the mildness of the bell peppers and the intensity of the capers and anchovies. It is stupendous with a robust roast lamb, and a superb counterpoint to mild white-fleshed fish as well.

20 red bell peppers

5 tablespoons extra virgin olive oil

6 garlic cloves, crushed and peeled

½ cup finely chopped Spanish onion

4 anchovies, finely chopped

2 tablespoons fresh thyme leaves

Sea or kosher salt and freshly ground black pepper

2 tablespoons granulated sugar

2 tablespoons red wine vinegar

2 tablespoons drained capers

2 tablespoons finely chopped fresh flat-leaf parsley

• Prepare a "mature and level" coal bed (see page 90), with a clean thin grate or rack set over it if desired, or preheat a grill to high.

• Put the red peppers on the coals or grill grate and cook, turning every few minutes, until blackened on all sides. Transfer to a large bowl, cover tightly with plastic wrap, and let steam and cool for 20 minutes.

• Peel the peppers by scraping off the skin with the back of a knife and remove the cores and seeds. Cut into ½-inch dice.

• Heat ¼ cup of the olive oil in a medium saucepan over medium-low heat. Add the garlic and cook just until golden brown, 2 to 3 minutes. Add the onion, anchovies, and thyme, season with salt and pepper, and cook until the onion is just golden, 4 to 5 minutes. Add the diced red peppers and sugar, stir to combine, and cook for 2 minutes. Add the red wine vinegar and cook until it has evaporated and the pan is dry. Taste and adjust the seasoning if necessary.

• Using an immersion blender, blitz the mixture for 3 seconds, or just until coarsely pureed; the spackle should still be chunky. Or transfer to a regular blender and pulse to a coarse puree.

• Spread the mixture in an even ½-inch-thick layer on a parchment-lined dehydrator tray (or trays) and dry in a dehydrator at 105°F for 3 hours, or until the consistency of tomato paste. Alternatively, spread on a parchment-lined baking sheet, put in a convection oven set at the lowest setting, prop the door ajar with the handle of a wooden spoon, and dry for 3 hours, or until the spackle is the consistency of tomato paste.

• Using a rubber spatula, scrape the spackle into a bowl or other container. Stir in the capers and parsley and the remaining 1 tablespoon olive oil. The spackle can be used right away, but for the best flavor, refrigerate in a tightly sealed container for at least a day, or up to 4 days, before using.

MANGO SPACKLE

Makes 5 cups

My riff on the classic Major Grey's mango chutney. By combining fresh mango chunks with lightly caramelized diced mango, you get the whole spectrum of mango-ness. The combination of fresh fruit with a chutney of the same fruit—sweet, sour, salty, aromatically spiced, and savory—is a wonderfully complete complement to perfectly grilled food.

5 tablespoons extra virgin olive oil

6 garlic cloves, crushed and peeled

½ cup finely chopped red onion

1 tablespoon grated ginger

1 tablespoon Madras curry powder

Sea or kosher salt and freshly ground black pepper

2 tablespoons granulated sugar

6 cups ½-inch dice ripe mango (about 2 large mangoes)

2 tablespoons rice wine vinegar

½ cup Major Grey's mango chutney

¼ cup sliced scallions

2 tablespoons freshly squeezed lime juice

½ cup finely chopped fresh cilantro

• Heat ¼ cup of the olive oil in a medium saucepan over medium-low heat. Add the garlic and cook just until golden brown, 2 to 3 minutes. Add the onion, ginger, and curry powder, season with salt and pepper, and cook until the onion is just golden, 4 to 5 minutes. Add the sugar and diced mango, stir to combine, and cook for 4 minutes. Add the rice wine vinegar and cook until it has evaporated and the pan is dry, then add the chutney, scallions, and lime juice and cook for 2 minutes. Taste and adjust the seasoning if necessary.

• Using an immersion blender, blitz the mixture for 3 seconds, or just until coarsely pureed; the spackle should still be chunky. Or transfer to a regular blender and pulse to a coarse puree.

• Spread the mixture in an even ½-inch-thick layer on a parchment-lined dehydrator tray (or trays) and dry in a dehydrator at 105°F for 3 hours, or until the consistency of tomato paste. Alternatively, spread on a parchment-lined baking sheet, put in a convection oven set at the lowest setting, prop the door ajar with the handle of a wooden spoon, and dry for 3 hours, or until the spackle is the consistency of tomato paste.

• Using a rubber spatula, scrape the spackle into a bowl or other container. Stir in the cilantro and the remaining 1 tablespoon olive oil. The spackle can be used right away, but for the best flavor, refrigerate in a tightly sealed container for at least a day, or up to 4 days, before using.

CRANBERRY SPACKLE

Makes 3 cups

Why is it that we eat cranberries at Thanksgiving and then forget about them the rest of the year? After all, we eat fruit preserves, applesauce, pickles, and relishes long after their harvest seasons. For wild game, intense dark meats, and full-flavored salmon, tuna, or mackerel this finisher is good year round. It also makes a change with a plate of long-cooked beans. Marjoram and rosemary add a subtle floral accent and pomegranate juice lends pucker to the mostly bitter, slight sweetness of cranberries. I don't cook the cranberries down to a red mush that looks like chopped raw sirloin. Instead, I leave them on the fire just until the heat bursts the skin but the fruit is still semi-whole, then dry the cranberries intact to concentrate the flavor.

1 cup granulated sugar

2 fresh rosemary sprigs

¼ cup Original Moonshine clear corn whiskey or vodka

¾ cup pomegranate juice

2 tablespoons fresh lime juice

½ cup water

4 cups (1 pound) fresh cranberries

1 tablespoon fresh lemon thyme leaves

1 tablespoon fresh marjoram leaves

1 tablespoon grated orange zest

Sea or kosher salt and freshly ground black pepper

2 tablespoons finely chopped fresh flat-leaf parsley

1 tablespoon extra virgin olive oil

• Combine the sugar, rosemary, and spirits in a medium saucepan and cook over medium-low heat until the alcohol burns off, a minute or so. Add the pomegranate juice, lime juice, and water and bring to a boil. Drop in the cranberries, reduce the heat to a simmer, and cook until the cranberries are soft and tender, 25 to 35 minutes.

• Add the lemon thyme, marjoram, and orange zest, remove from the heat, cover, and allow to stand for 20 minutes.

• Season the cranberry mixture with salt and pepper and drain in a sieve set over a small saucepan. Transfer the cranberries to a bowl. Bring the liquid to a boil and boil until reduced to a syrup, then stir into the cranberries.

- Spread the mixture in an even ½-inch-thick layer on a parchment-lined dehydrator tray (or trays) and dry in a dehydrator at 105°F for 3 hours, or until the consistency of tomato paste. Alternatively, spread on a parchment-lined baking sheet, put in a convection oven set at the lowest setting, prop the door ajar with the handle of a wooden spoon, and dry for 3 hours, or until the spackle is the consistency of tomato paste.

- Using a rubber spatula, scrape the spackle into a bowl or other container. Stir in the parsley and the olive oil. The spackle can be used right away, but for the best flavor, refrigerate in a tightly sealed container for at least a day, or up to 4 days, before using.

TOMATO SPACKLE

Makes approximately 2½ cups

I grew up thinking that there were two kinds of tomato preparations used for finishers. The first was ketchup, which I know many people love, but it's not one of my favorites. The second was tomato jelly, which is something that is often presented as a house gift, and then, years later, you end up saying, "Hey, honey, this has been on the shelf since 2004. Is it OK to get rid of it?"

This spackle is as intense as ketchup but so much more layered and nuanced in flavor—just as things usually are when you make them from scratch.

3 tablespoons extra virgin olive oil

5 garlic cloves, crushed and peeled

½ cup finely chopped Spanish onion

1 teaspoon sea or kosher salt, or to taste

2 tablespoons tomato paste

5 cups coarsely chopped drained canned tomatoes

1 cup chopped drained sun-dried tomatoes packed in oil

2 tablespoons red wine vinegar

1 teaspoon dried oregano

1 tablespoon granulated sugar

1 teaspoon garlic salt

Freshly ground black pepper

¼ cup finely chopped fresh flat-leaf parsley

• Heat 2 tablespoons of the olive oil in a large saucepan over medium heat until hot. Add the garlic and cook until lightly browned, about 2 minutes. Add the onion, season with the salt, and cook until translucent, about 3 minutes.

• Add the tomato paste and cook, stirring, for 1 minute. Add the canned and sun-dried tomatoes, red wine vinegar, oregano, sugar, and garlic salt and cook until the tomatoes have broken down and the juices are reduced by half, about 10 minutes. Season with pepper to taste and additional salt if necessary.

• Using an immersion blender, blitz the mixture for 3 seconds, or just until coarsely pureed; the spackle should still be chunky. Or transfer to a regular blender and pulse to a coarse puree.

- Spread the mixture in an even ½-inch-thick layer on a parchment-lined dehydrator tray (or trays) and dry in a dehydrator at 105°F for 3 hours, or until the consistency of tomato paste. Alternatively, spread on a parchment-lined baking sheet, put in a convection oven set at the lowest setting, prop the door ajar with the handle of a wooden spoon, and dry for 3 hours, or until the spackle is the consistency of tomato paste.

- Using a rubber spatula, scrape the spackle into a bowl or other container. Stir in the parsley and the remaining 1 tablespoon olive oil. The spackle can be used right away, but for the best flavor, refrigerate in a tightly sealed container for at least a day, or up to 4 days, before using.

ARTICHOKE SPACKLE

Makes approximately 2 cups

This finisher is a superconcentrated variation of *barigoule,* the classic Provençal dish of artichokes braised with aromatics in white wine. I find that adding in green tomato jam contributes sweetness and tanginess, bridges all the flavors, and provides body to bind the spackle together. Powerful in taste, it is light and earthy at the same time. It's best with chicken or fish.

7 medium artichokes

1 lemon, halved

3 tablespoons extra virgin olive oil

3 garlic cloves, crushed and peeled

½ teaspoon sea or kosher salt

⅛ teaspoon freshly ground black pepper

¼ cup finely chopped Spanish onion

2 tablespoons finely chopped carrot

¼ cup dry white wine

½ teaspoon anchovy paste

½ tablespoon drained capers

4 ounces green tomato jam

½ cup water

2 tablespoons coarsely chopped drained sun-dried tomatoes packed in oil

5 fresh basil leaves, cut into 3 pieces each

1 tablespoon finely chopped fresh flat-leaf parsley

- To trim the artichokes to hearts, cut off the stem of each one; as you work, rub the cut surfaces of the artichokes with one of the lemons halves to keep them from darkening. Break off the tough outer leaves until you reach the pale yellow inner cone of leaves. Cut off the cone of leaves, pull out any small purple leaves, and, using a sharp spoon, scoop out the fuzzy choke. Trim off all the dark green parts of the bottom of the artichoke heart. Cut the hearts into ½-inch cubes and toss with the juice of the remaining lemon half.

- Heat 2 tablespoons of the olive oil in a large skillet over medium-high heat until hot. Add the garlic and artichokes, tossing to coat with oil, season with the salt and pepper, and cook until lightly golden, about 5 minutes. Reduce the heat to medium-low, add the onion and carrot, and cook until beginning to soften, about 3 minutes.

- Add the white wine, anchovy paste, capers, and tomato jam, bring to a simmer over medium heat, and cook until the wine has evaporated and the oil is starting to crackle. Add the water and bring just to a boil, then cover, reduce the heat to a simmer, and cook until the artichokes are tender, 20 to 25 minutes. Remove the lid and cook until most of the remaining liquid has evaporated.

- Using an immersion blender, blitz the mixture for 3 seconds, or just until coarsely pureed; the spackle should still be chunky. Or transfer to a regular blender and pulse to a coarse puree. Stir the sun-dried tomatoes into the puree.

- Spread the mixture in an even ½-inch-thick layer on a parchment-lined dehydrator tray (or trays) and dry in a dehydrator at 105°F for 3 hours, or until the consistency of tomato paste. Alternatively, spread on a parchment-lined baking sheet, put in a convection oven set at the lowest setting, prop the door ajar with the handle of a wooden spoon, and dry for 3 hours, or until the spackle is the consistency of tomato paste.

- Using a rubber spatula, scrape the spackle into a bowl or other container. Stir in the basil, parsley, and the remaining 1 tablespoon extra virgin olive oil. The spackle can be used right away, but for the best flavor, refrigerate in a tightly sealed container for at least a day, or up to 4 days, before using.

HATCH CHILE SPACKLE

Makes 3 cups

Years ago, when I was traveling around America on my Holy Grail/Barbecue Quest, I found myself in the town of Hatch, New Mexico, where I ran into a cowboy who had a mound of chiles that he was stuffing into Ziploc bags. I asked him what he was doing with so many chiles. He told me that they were a very special chile, available only once a year, and the local tradition was to roast them and then freeze them to have on hand year round.

I was extremely interested, so I invited myself along when he took his sack of chiles to the parking lot of the local version of a Winn-Dixie store. He handed his treasure to some folks who heaved them into a giant chile roaster that looked like a cement mixer connected to a blowtorch. After approximately ten minutes, the chiles were returned in a sack, as sweet, charred, *picante* steam filtered through the burlap. Fresh out of the roaster, the taste was smoky, herbaceous, and beautifully concentrated—perfect as a spackle base.

If you can't get fresh green chiles from Hatch, New Mexico, you can order frozen online (see Sources, page 256); substitute 3 cups chopped chiles for the fresh. Or make the recipe with poblano chiles—the result will be somewhat different but still good.

15 to 20 Hatch green chiles

5 tablespoons extra virgin olive oil

6 garlic cloves, crushed and peeled

½ cup finely chopped Spanish onion

1 teaspoon garlic salt

2 tablespoons fresh thyme leaves

Sea or kosher salt and freshly ground black pepper

2 tablespoons granulated sugar

2 tablespoons white wine vinegar

2 tablespoons finely chopped fresh cilantro

• Prepare a "mature and level" coal bed (see page 90), with a clean thin grate or rack set over it if desired, or preheat a grill to high.

• Put the chiles on the coals or grill grate and cook, turning every few minutes, until blackened on all sides. Transfer to a large bowl, cover tightly with plastic wrap, and let steam and cool for 20 minutes.

• Peel the chiles by scraping off the skin with the back of a knife and remove the cores and seeds. Cut into ½-inch dice—you should have about 3 cups.

- Heat ¼ cup of the olive oil in a medium saucepan over medium-low heat. Add the garlic and cook just until golden brown, 2 to 3 minutes. Add the onion, garlic salt, and thyme, season with salt and pepper, and cook until the onion is just golden, 4 to 5 minutes. Add the diced chiles and sugar, stir to combine, and cook for 2 minutes. Add the white wine vinegar and cook until it has evaporated and the pan is dry. Taste and adjust the seasoning if necessary.

- Using an immersion blender, blitz the mixture for 3 seconds, or just until coarsely pureed; the spackle should still be chunky. Or transfer to a regular blender and pulse to a coarse puree.

- Spread the mixture in an even ½-inch-thick layer on a parchment-lined dehydrator tray (or trays) and dry in a dehydrator at 105°F for 3 hours, or until the consistency of tomato paste. Alternatively, spread on a parchment-lined baking sheet, put in a convection oven set at the lowest setting, prop the door ajar with the handle of a wooden spoon, and dry for 3 hours, or until the spackle is the consistency of tomato paste.

- Using a rubber spatula, scrape the spackle into a bowl or other container. Stir in the cilantro and the remaining 1 tablespoon olive oil. The spackle can be used right away, but for the best flavor, refrigerate in a tightly sealed container for at least a day, or up to 4 days, before using.

CONCENTRATED CAPONATA

Makes approximately 4 cups

I love the sweet, piquant, and savory eggplant salad known as caponata. It's like amped-up ratatouille, but long-roasted, with more concentrated sweet-and-sour flavor. This fork finisher takes it to the next step. The eggplant is floured and fried, then tempered in vinegar and showered with tons of parsley. Great with rib eye or lamb, or even alone with crusty bread.

4 cups olive oil

1 eggplant, peeled and cut into ½-inch cubes

1 tablespoon sea or kosher salt, or to taste

1 teaspoon freshly ground black pepper, or to taste

1 cup all-purpose flour

3 tablespoons extra virgin olive oil

5 garlic cloves, crushed and peeled

½ cup finely chopped Spanish onion

1 cup finely chopped celery

1 teaspoon anchovy paste

1 tablespoon tomato paste

2 cups coarsely chopped drained canned tomatoes

2 tablespoons drained capers

2 tablespoons dried currants

15 green olives, such as Cerignola, pitted and coarsely chopped

1 teaspoon dried oregano

1 tablespoon granulated sugar

2 teaspoons garlic salt

2 tablespoons red wine vinegar

¼ cup finely chopped fresh flat-leaf parsley

• Heat the 4 cups olive oil in a medium pot over medium-high heat until it sizzles when a pinch of flour is dropped into it. Meanwhile, season the eggplant with 2 teaspoons of the salt and the pepper, then toss with the flour, shaking off the excess.

• Working in batches, add the eggplant to the hot oil and fry until golden brown, about 3 minutes. Remove with a slotted spoon and drain on paper towels.

• Heat 2 tablespoons of the extra virgin olive oil in a large saucepan over medium heat. Add the garlic and cook until lightly browned, about 2 minutes. Add the onion, celery, and the remaining 1 teaspoon salt and cook until the onion is translucent and the celery is tender, about 5 minutes.

• Add the anchovy paste and tomato paste and cook, stirring, for 1 minute. Add the tomatoes, bring to a simmer, and cook until the tomatoes are broken down and the juices are reduced by half, about 10 minutes.

- Add the capers, currants, olives, oregano, sugar, and garlic salt, then stir in the fried eggplant and cook for 10 minutes. Add the vinegar and adjust the seasoning if necessary.

- Using an immersion blender, blitz the mixture for 3 seconds, or just until coarsely pureed; the spackle should still be chunky. Or transfer to a regular blender and pulse to a coarse puree.

- Spread the mixture in an even ½-inch-thick layer on a parchment-lined dehydrator tray (or trays) and dry in a dehydrator at 105°F for 3 hours, or until the consistency of tomato paste. Alternatively, spread on a parchment-lined baking sheet, put in a convection oven set at the lowest setting, prop the door ajar with the handle of a wooden spoon, and dry for 3 hours, or until the caponata is the consistency of tomato paste.

- Using a rubber spatula, scrape the caponata into a bowl or other container. Stir in the parsley and the remaining 1 tablespoon extra virgin olive oil. The caponata can be used right away, but for the best flavor, refrigerate in a tightly sealed container for at least a day, or up to 4 days, before using.

BASTES

Every time you season, turn, slice, or serve a piece of meat, you have an opportunity to develop flavor. My bastes build layer upon layer of flavor. They also do much more than that. Because they are cooler than the meat to which they are applied, they temper and soften the outer crust. Of course, the interior of the meat doesn't have a clue this is happening. It just keeps driving the temperature up as heat penetrates to the center.

The fat in the baste also crisps the meat proteins as the liquid cooks out, helping to build crust with every application. I think of a Japanese lacquered box, where layer upon layer is added to produce a depth of finish that is more beautiful than one coat of lacquer could ever be.

Depending on how long I am cooking a piece of meat, or how intense the heat, I may vary how much fat (butter, meat trimmings, oil) I use and how much liquid (water, vinegar, lemon juice, wine). Again, the liquid tempers the meat, but in addition, as it reduces, the baste leaves behind strictly concentrated flavor that lightly permeates the crust and the layer of meat just under the crust.

My bastes, in concert with my Finishing Salts (see page 240), are based on combinations of sweet, sour, salty, and hot. So is every barbecue sauce ever invented. I grew up loving those sauces, but as a chef, at times I prefer the simplicity and directness of my own bastes. They give me more control over flavor and texture and more opportunities to adjust: from seasoning before cooking until the moment that the fateful forkful goes into your mouth.

In many cases, I have not recommended specific bastes for the recipes in this book. It really is a matter of what you feel like: they can be used interchangeably.

Note that all of the bastes used here are applied with an herb brush (see page 8).

I also include brines, which add flavor and preserve juiciness. Finally, of course, you can't do a barbecue book without barbecue sauce—so try my homemade favorite.

230   Basic Baste

231   Lemon Oregano Baste

232   Lemon, Garlic, and Herbes de
Provence Baste

233   Chimichurri Baste

234   Classic Southern Baste

234   Butter Baste

237   Habanero Syrup

237   BBQ Sauce

238   Basic Brine

238   Very Basic Brine

BASIC BASTE

Makes approximately 4 cups (if using the acid component)

FAT BASTE

1¼ cups extra virgin olive oil

10 tablespoons (1¼ sticks) unsalted butter

½ cup rendered fat from the meat being cooked (optional)

1 tablespoon soy sauce

1 tablespoon granulated sugar

2 tablespoons grated garlic (use a Microplane) or garlic mashed to a paste

1 tablespoon fresh thyme leaves

2 tablespoons grated Spanish onion (use a Microplane)

2 teaspoons sea or kosher salt

2 teaspoons freshly ground black pepper

1 teaspoon red pepper flakes

ACID COMPONENT (OPTIONAL)

¼ cup freshly squeezed lemon juice

¼ cup white wine vinegar

• Combine all the ingredients for the fat baste in a 2-quart saucepan and bring just to a simmer; remove from the heat. For the best flavor, refrigerate in a tightly sealed container for 1 to 2 days (reheat over low heat to melt the butter before using).

• For recipes that use the optional acid component, whisk it into the fat baste before using, or reserve it to add later, as specified in the individual recipe.

THESE RECIPES BREAK EVERY BASTE DOWN INTO TWO PARTS

1. The fat baste serves to temper, develop crust, and build flavor. This is the baste I use to build a crust quickly on smaller cuts of meat.
2. The acid component option calls for the addition of a tangy liquid. I use these only in longer, multiple-baste recipes for larger pieces of meat. The vinegar, wine, or lemon juice contributes additional tempering, concentrates flavor as the liquid reduces, and hydrates the crust so that it doesn't dry out and overly harden. At the same time, applying small amounts of the baste numerous times during cooking means there is never so much liquid that the crust becomes soggy.

LEMON OREGANO BASTE

Makes approximately 4 cups (if using the acid component)

FAT BASTE

1¼ cups extra virgin olive oil

10 tablespoons (1¼ sticks) unsalted butter

½ cup rendered fat from the meat being cooked (optional)

1 tablespoon granulated sugar

2 tablespoons grated garlic (use a Microplane) or garlic mashed to a paste

2 tablespoons grated Spanish onion (use a Microplane)

¼ cup grated red bell pepper (use a Microplane)

¼ cup grated celery (use a Microplane)

2 tablespoons dried oregano

2 teaspoons sea or kosher salt

2 teaspoons freshly ground black pepper

1 teaspoon red pepper flakes

ACID COMPONENT (OPTIONAL)

¼ cup freshly squeezed lemon juice

¼ cup white wine vinegar

- Combine all the ingredients for the fat baste in a 2-quart saucepan and bring just to a simmer; remove from the heat. For the best flavor, refrigerate in a tightly sealed container for 1 to 2 days (reheat over low heat to melt the butter before using).

- For recipes that use the optional acid component, whisk it into the fat baste before using, or reserve it to add later, as specified in the individual recipe.

LEMON, GARLIC, AND HERBES DE PROVENCE BASTE

Makes approximately 4 cups (if using the acid component)

FAT BASTE

1¼ cups extra virgin olive oil

10 tablespoons (1¼ sticks) unsalted butter

½ cup rendered fat from the meat being cooked (optional)

1 tablespoon granulated sugar

2 tablespoons grated garlic (use a Microplane) or garlic mashed to a paste

2 tablespoons grated Spanish onion (use a Microplane)

1 tablespoon dried oregano

1 tablespoon dried lavender

1 tablespoon fresh rosemary leaves

1 tablespoon fresh thyme leaves

1 tablespoon fresh flat-leaf parsley leaves

2 teaspoons sea or kosher salt

2 teaspoons freshly ground black pepper

1 teaspoon red pepper flakes

ACID COMPONENT (OPTIONAL)

¼ cup white wine vinegar

¼ cup freshly squeezed lemon juice

- Combine all the ingredients for the fat baste in a 2-quart saucepan and bring just to a simmer; remove from the heat. For the best flavor, refrigerate in a tightly sealed container for 1 to 2 days (reheat over low heat to melt the butter before using).

- For recipes that use the optional acid component, whisk it into the fat baste before using, or reserve it to add later, as specified in the individual recipe.

CHIMICHURRI BASTE

Makes approximately 4 cups (if using the acid component)

FAT BASTE

1¼ cups extra virgin olive oil

10 tablespoons (1¼ sticks) unsalted butter

½ cup rendered fat from the meat being cooked (optional)

1 tablespoon granulated sugar

1 tablespoon grated garlic (use a **Microplane**) or garlic mashed to a paste

1 tablespoon dried oregano

1 teaspoon ground cumin

2 teaspoons sea or kosher salt

2 teaspoons freshly ground black pepper

1 teaspoon red pepper flakes

¼ cup chopped fresh flat-leaf parsley

¼ cup chopped fresh cilantro

ACID COMPONENT (OPTIONAL)

½ cup white wine vinegar

• Combine all the ingredients for the fat baste in a 2-quart saucepan and bring just to a simmer; remove from the heat. For the best flavor, refrigerate in a tightly sealed container for 1 to 2 days (reheat over low heat to melt the butter before using).

• For recipes that use the optional acid component, whisk it into the fat baste before using, or reserve it to add later, as specified in the individual recipe.

CLASSIC SOUTHERN BASTE

Makes approximately 3 cups (if using the acid component)

FAT BASTE

1¼ cups extra virgin olive oil

10 tablespoons (1¼ sticks)
unsalted butter

½ cup rendered fat from the meat
being cooked (optional)

1 teaspoon soy sauce

1 teaspoon Worcestershire sauce

1 tablespoon dark brown sugar

2 tablespoons grated garlic
(use a Microplane) or garlic mashed
to a paste

1 tablespoon fresh thyme leaves

2 tablespoons grated Spanish onion
(use a Microplane)

2 teaspoons sea or kosher salt

2 teaspoons freshly ground
black pepper

1 teaspoon red pepper flakes

ACID COMPONENT (OPTIONAL)

½ cup cider vinegar

1 tablespoon ketchup

1 tablespoon yellow mustard

• Combine all the ingredients for the fat baste in a 2-quart saucepan and bring just to a simmer; remove from the heat. For the best flavor, refrigerate in a tightly sealed container for 1 to 2 days (reheat over low heat to melt the butter before using).

• For recipes that use the optional acid component, whisk it into the fat baste before using, or reserve it to add later, as specified in the individual recipe.

BUTTER BASTE

Makes 1 cup

½ pound (2 sticks) unsalted butter,
cut into chunks

5 garlic cloves, crushed and peeled

½ teaspoon red pepper flakes

1 tablespoon fresh thyme leaves

• Combine all the ingredients in a medium saucepan and heat over medium heat until the butter melts, then bring just to a simmer and simmer gently for 2 to 4 minutes. Let stand for at least 1 hour to bring out the flavors.

• Reheat over low heat to melt the butter before using.

HABANERO SYRUP

Makes approximately 1½ cups

1 cup granulated sugar

½ cup water

1 habanero pepper, seeded and
finely chopped

2 garlic cloves, crushed and peeled

¼ cup finely chopped scallions

Juice of 1 lime

- Combine the sugar, water, habanero, and garlic in a small saucepan and bring
  to a simmer, stirring to dissolve the sugar. Remove from the heat and stir in
  the scallions and lime juice. Let stand for at least 1 hour before using to bring
  out the flavors. The syrup can be refrigerated in a covered container for up to
  1 week.

BBQ SAUCE

Makes approximately 4 cups

½ cup vegetable oil

5 garlic cloves, crushed and peeled

2 teaspoons garlic salt

1 tablespoon chili powder

1 cup packed light brown sugar

2 cups water

2 cups ketchup

½ cup unsulfured blackstrap molasses

½ cup cider vinegar

1 teaspoon Worcestershire sauce

½ cup yellow mustard

¼ cup red pepper jelly

¼ teaspoon liquid smoke

- Combine the oil and garlic in a medium pot and cook over low heat, stirring
  occasionally, until the garlic is lightly golden, 2 to 3 minutes. Add the garlic
  salt, chili powder, and brown sugar and cook, stirring constantly, for 1 minute.

- Add the water, ketchup, molasses, vinegar, Worcestershire sauce, mustard,
  pepper jelly, and liquid smoke and bring to a boil. Reduce the heat and
  simmer gently, stirring frequently to prevent burning, until reduced to 4 cups,
  20 to 30 minutes. Remove from the heat and allow to cool. The sauce will
  keep, refrigerated in an airtight container, for up to 1 week.

BASIC BRINE

Makes approximately 8 cups

8 cups water

¼ cup sea or kosher salt

2 tablespoons granulated sugar

2 lemons, cut in half

3 bay leaves, preferably fresh

8 garlic cloves, crushed and peeled

2 tablespoons fresh thyme leaves

1 tablespoon black peppercorns

1 teaspoon red pepper flakes

• Combine all the ingredients in a large saucepan and bring to a boil over high heat. Transfer to a bowl or other container and allow to cool, then refrigerate overnight before using.

VERY BASIC BRINE

Makes approximately 5 cups

¼ cup sea or kosher salt

3 cups water

2 cups apple juice

10 garlic cloves, crushed and peeled

1 tablespoon coarsely ground black pepper

• Combine all the ingredients in a medium saucepan and bring to a boil over high heat. Transfer to a bowl or other container and allow to cool, then refrigerate overnight before using.

FINISHING SALTS

The great American chef Thomas Keller is famous with his kitchen workers for his unshakable commandment that "no liquid can move from one container to another without passing through a strainer." His belief is that it makes for ever-increasing clarity and distinction of flavor.

I have a similar sentiment every time I move to the next step in the cooking process. I look to see if it has the potential of piggybacking even more flavor. For example, seasoning with salt, all by itself, adds a ton of flavor, elevating every other taste and flavor in a recipe. So far, so good, but why stop there? What can you do to salt that will create even more flavor? Surprising flavor? Flavor that elegantly finishes the recipe you have worked so carefully to prepare?

I have grown partial to the technique of moistening salt with a liquid such as vinegar, lime or lemon juice, or wine, then adding herbs and/ or spices, or even ashes. As the wet salt dries out and recrystallizes in a dehydrator or low oven, it incorporates intense flavors from the liquids and other ingredients.

244 Thyme, Rosemary, and
Sage Salt

245 Mint, Lemon, and
Rosemary Salt

246 Lemon Thyme Salt

248 Lime Coriander Salt

250 Thyme Zinfandel Salt

251 Wine Vinegar Salt

252 Worcestershire Salt

253 Charcoal Salt

THYME, ROSEMARY, AND SAGE SALT

Makes approximately 1 cup

These classic herbs, used separately or together, carry a powerful perfume. The salt captures their volatile oils so that they are experienced as freshly released flavor rather than simply as a pleasant aroma that precedes the tasting experience.

1 cup sea or kosher salt

1 tablespoon fresh thyme leaves

1 tablespoon fresh rosemary leaves

1 tablespoon thinly slivered (chiffonade) fresh sage leaves

1 teaspoon ground fennel

½ teaspoon ground juniper berries

- Combine all the ingredients in a bowl and mash them with your fingers to mix the herbs in with the salt.

- Spread the mixture out in a thin, even layer on a parchment-lined dehydrator tray and dry in a dehydrater at 105°F for 12 hours. Alternatively, spread the mixture on a parchment-lined baking sheet, put in a convection oven at the lowest setting, prop the door ajar with the handle of a wooden spoon, and let dry completely, about 12 hours.

- Finely grind in a spice grinder or clean coffee grinder and dry for another 2 hours.

- Store in an airtight container at room temperature for up to 1 month.

MINT, LEMON, AND ROSEMARY SALT

Makes approximately 1 cup

I use this salt on grilled lamb. I take three of the most popular accompaniments for lamb and infuse salt with cool, clean mintiness, herbal tones from rosemary, and fruity acidity. If I simply squirted lemon juice on the lamb, it would make the crust soggy. Here I get flavor without the sog.

1 cup sea or kosher salt	1 teaspoon granulated sugar
1 tablespoon grated lemon zest	1 tablespoon crushed dried mint
⅓ cup freshly squeezed lemon juice	1 tablespoon dried rosemary

• Combine the salt, zest, juice, and sugar in a bowl, stirring until slushy.

• Spread the salt mixture out in a thin, even layer on a parchment-lined dehydrator tray and dry in a dehydrator at 105°F for 12 hours. Alternatively, spread the mixture on a parchment-lined baking sheet, put in a convection oven set at the lowest setting, prop the door ajar with the handle of a wooden spoon, and let dry completely, about 12 hours.

• Finely grind in a spice grinder or clean coffee grinder and dry for another 2 hours.

• Transfer the salt mixture back to the grinder, add the dried mint and rosemary, and pulse to the consistency of sand. Store in an airtight container at room temperature for up to 1 month.

LEMON THYME SALT

Makes approximately 1 cup

A fresh floral herb gets the tang of slightly floral lemon—and then a boost of extra power from the flavor-enhancing salt.

1 cup sea or kosher salt

⅓ cup freshly squeezed lemon juice

1 tablespoon grated lemon zest

1 tablespoon fresh thyme leaves

- Combine the salt, zest, and juice in a bowl, stirring until slushy.

- Spread the salt mixture out in a thin, even layer on a parchment-lined dehydrator tray and dry in a dehydrator at 105°F for 12 hours. Alternatively, spread the mixture on a parchment-lined baking sheet, put in a convection oven set at the lowest setting, prop the door ajar with the handle of a wooden spoon, and let dry completely, about 12 hours.

- Finely grind in a spice grinder or clean coffee grinder and dry for another 2 hours.

- Transfer the salt mixture back to the grinder, add the thyme, and pulse to the consistency of sand. Store in an airtight container at room temperature for up to 1 month.

LIME CORIANDER SALT

Makes approximately 1 cup

The combination of lime and salt works beautifully with other fruit—for example, sliced watermelon or mango. But one thing these fruits don't need is more water. Lime has all the flavor and none of the wetness. It is absolutely superb with savory dishes such as pulled pork. And coriander seed lends a spiced aromatic note that stands up well to the pork.

1 cup sea or kosher salt

1 tablespoon grated lime zest

⅓ cup freshly squeezed lime juice

1 tablespoon ground coriander seeds

1 tablespoon julienned chile peppers

• Combine the salt, zest, and juice in a bowl, stirring until slushy.

• Spread the salt mixture out in a thin, even layer on a parchment-lined dehydrator tray and dry in a dehydrator at 105°F for 12 hours. Alternatively, spread the mixture on a parchment-lined baking sheet, put in a convection oven set at the lowest setting, prop the door ajar with the handle of a wooden spoon, and let dry completely, about 12 hours.

• Finely grind in a spice grinder or clean coffee grinder and dry for another 2 hours.

• Transfer the salt mixture back to the grinder, add the ground coriander, and pulse to the consistency of sand. Mix in the chiles. Store in an airtight container at room temperature for up to 1 month.

THYME ZINFANDEL SALT

Makes approximately 1 cup

I knew a Tuscan butcher, Dario, who was a huge, powerful guy, the kind who lifts you off the floor when he gives you a hug. He made the first herb salt I ever tasted, *perfumo del Chianti* (named for the region, not the wine). It was so delicious that it inspired this recipe and these other seasoning salts (the herbs certainly added to that impression). When I first tried this one and tasted the result, I swear I would have kept looking for the rest of the coq au vin if I hadn't known better. I even imagined for a second that I heard Julia Child chuckling in my kitchen—standing over a hot stove for ten hours sometimes has a hallucinatory effect like that.

1 cup sea or kosher salt **1 tablespoon dried thyme**
⅓ cup zinfandel

• Combine the salt and wine in a bowl, stirring until slushy.

• Spread the salt mixture out in a thin, even layer on a parchment-lined dehydrator tray and dry in a dehydrator at 105°F for 12 hours. Alternatively, spread the mixture on a parchment-lined baking sheet, put in a convection oven set at the lowest setting, prop the door ajar with the handle of a wooden spoon, and let dry completely, about 12 hours.

• Finely grind in a spice grinder or clean coffee grinder and dry for another 2 hours.

• Transfer the salt mixture back to the grinder, add the dried thyme, and pulse to the consistency of sand. Store in an airtight container at room temperature for up to 1 month.

WINE VINEGAR SALT

Makes approximately 1 cup

While spending time in England, I've learned that the English love salt and vinegar on their potato crisps, or, as we call them, potato chips. They are also partial to the same combination on their batter-fried fish. By infusing the vinegar into the salt, I get all the flavor but none of the sogginess that defeats a golden crust. Wine vinegar, rather than cider vinegar or white vinegar, contributes a hint of floral fruit.

1 cup sea or kosher salt   **⅓ cup red or white wine vinegar**

- Combine the salt and vinegar in a bowl, stirring until slushy.

- Spread the salt mixture out in a thin, even layer on a parchment-lined dehydrator tray and dry in a dehydrator at 105°F for 12 hours. Alternatively, spread the mixture on a parchment-lined baking sheet, put in a convection oven set at the lowest setting, prop the door ajar with the handle of a wooden spoon, and let dry completely, about 12 hours.

- Finely grind in a spice grinder or clean coffee grinder and dry for another 2 hours.

- Transfer the spice mixture back to the grinder and pulse to the consistency of sand. Store in an airtight container at room temperature for up to 1 month.

WORCESTERSHIRE SALT

Makes approximately 1 cup

Like the Wine Vinegar Salt (page 251) and chips, this idea came from the way that the English love to match up Worcestershire sauce with beef. So do I.

1 cup sea or kosher salt
1 cup Worcestershire sauce

1 tablespoon freshly ground
black pepper

- Combine the salt and Worcestershire sauce in a bowl, stirring until slushy.

- Spread the salt mixture out in a thin, even layer on a parchment-lined dehydrator tray and dry in a dehydrator at 105°F for 12 hours. Or, spread on a parchment-lined baking sheet, put in a convection oven set at the lowest setting, prop the door ajar with a wooden spoon, and let dry completely.

- Finely grind in a spice grinder or clean coffee grinder and dry for another 2 hours.

- Transfer back to the grinder, add the pepper, and pulse to the consistency of fine sand. Store in an airtight container at room temperature for up to 1 month.

CHARCOAL SALT

Makes approximately 1 cup

Tastes better than it sounds—way better. Just a little charcoal infuses everything with a hint of smoke, and the garlic adds a sweet, nutty finish.

1 cup sea or kosher salt

1 teaspoon garlic salt

A lump of good-quality hardwood lump charcoal, briefly rinsed and dried

- Combine the sea salt and garlic salt in a small bowl. Using a fine Microplane, grate about 1 tablespoon of the charcoal over the salt mixture. Using your fingertips, rub the charcoal into the salt until well combined.

- Transfer to a spice grinder or clean coffee grinder and pulse to the consistency of sand. Store in an airtight container at room temperature for up to 1 month.

Sea salt, garlic, and a soupçon of
grated hardwood charcoal result in a
unique finishing salt with a cool color.

SOURCES

Da Gift Baskets & Bags

www.dagiftbasket.com
Frozen, roasted, and peeled
Hatch chiles and a wide
range of other chiles and
Southwestern ingredients

D'Artagnan

www.dartagnan.com
Duck fat, magrets (duck
breasts), venison, and other
meats and game

ImportFood

www.importfood.com
A vast selection of Thai
ingredients, including
whole pickled garlic

JB Prince

www.jbprince.com
Knives and other high-
quality kitchen equipment

King Arthur Flour

www.kingarthurflour.com
Bread baker with domed lid

Microplane

www.microplane.com
High-quality graters
and zesters

Moonshine

www.moonshine.com
The Original Moonshine
Clear Corn Whiskey

Niman Ranch

www.nimanranch.com
Free-range and
organic meats

Penzey's Spices

www.penzeys.com
Sea salt, juniper berries,
and a vast range of
other spices

Sur La Table

www.surlatable.com
Dehydrators and other
kitchen equipment of
all kinds

La Tienda

www.tienda.com
Jarred piquillo peppers,
smoked anchovies, and
other Spanish ingredients

Weber

www.weber.com
Grills and accessories

INDEX

Note: Page numbers in *italics* refer to photographs.

acid, 208, 230

active grilling, xiii-xiv, 18

almonds:
  Peach and Nectarine Salad with
    Slivered Almonds, 168–69

anchovies:
  Watercress with Pickled Garlic and
    Smoked Anchovies, 184–85

apple(s):
  Green Apple, Cabbage, and Caraway
    Slaw, 162–63

Artichoke Spackle, 220–21

Arugula Salad with Lemon, Extra Virgin
    Olive Oil, and Parmesan Shavings,
    188

asparagus:
  Lemony Asparagus Shavings with
    Goat's-Milk-Curd Dressing, 170–71

avocado:
  Potato Cream with Leeks, Capers, and
    Avocado, 152–53

bacon:
  bacon envelope, *44–45*
  Bubbling Bacon Butter Beans,
    142–43
  Charred Radicchio with Sweet-and-
    Sticky Balsamic and Bacon, 178–79,
    180–81

baked beans:
  UKBB (United Kingdom Baked
    Beans), 144–45

balsamic vinegar:

bark, 2

Basic Baste, 230
  in Man Steak with Thyme Zinfandel
    Salt, 34, *35, 36,* 37

Basic Brine, 238
  in Clinched-and-Planked Chicken
    Legs, 124, 126, *127*
  in Clinched-and-Planked Shrimp, 110,
    111, 112

in Clinched Boneless Pork Chops,
    100–101

in Clinched Chicken Wingettes, 104–5

in Smoked Crack-Back Chicken with
    Lemon, Garlic, and Herbes de
    Provence Baste, 54–55, *56–57*

in Smoked Pork Shoulder with Lime
    Coriander Salt, 40–41

in Thick Pork Chops, Guaranteed Juicy,
    76–78

bastes, 226–39
  Basic Baste, 230
  Basic Brine, 238
  BBQ Sauce, 237
  broken into two parts, 230
  Butter Baste, 234
  Chimichurri Baste, 233
  Classic Southern Baste, 234
  Habanero Syrup, 237
  Lemon, Garlic, and Herbes de Provence
    Baste, 232
  Lemon Oregano Baste, 231
  Very Basic Brine, 238

basting, 12, 15, 25, *25*

Batali, Mario, 170

BBQ Sauce, 237

beans:
  Bubbling Bacon Butter Beans, 142–43
  UKBB (United Kingdom Baked Beans),
    144–45

beef:
  Clinched-and-Planked Rump Steaks,
    116–17
  Clinched Beef Tenderloin, 98–99
  Clinched Strip Steak, 92, *93,* 94
  clinching method, 91
  côte de boeuf (cowboy cut), 62
  Filet Mignon, 68–69
  High-Low Boneless Rib Eye, 62–63,
    64–65
  High-Low Center-Cut Tenderloin
    (aka Chateaubriand), 66–67

beef (*cont.*)
 Man Steak with Thyme Zinfandel Salt,
  34, *35, 36,* 37
 New York strip, 92
 Rib Roast Done Like a Steak, 71–72,
  74–75
 Smoked Brisket on the Bone with
  Chimichurri Crust, 48–49
beet greens:
 Baby Beet Greens and Mâche with
  Balsamic and Shaved Pecorino, 190
Belgian Endive Salad with Burnt
  Oranges, Marjoram Dressing, and
  Pomegranate Seeds, 186–87
beurre manié, 138, *139*
Bianco, Chris, 5
bitter greens, 174
Board Dressing, 27, *49*
 in Clinched-and-Planked Chicken
  Legs, 124, 126, *127*
 in Clinched-and-Planked Duck
  Breasts, 128–29
 in Clinched-and-Planked Game
  Steaks, 122–23
 in Clinched-and-Planked Lamb Racks,
  118–19, *120–21*
 in Clinched-and-Planked Rump
  Steaks, 116–17
 in Clinched Beef Tenderloin, 98–99
 in Clinched Boneless Pork Chops,
  100–101
 in Clinched Double-Wide Loin Lamb
  Chops, 102–3
 in Clinched Strip Steak, 92, *93,* 94
 in Double-Butterflied Leg of Lamb,
  50–51, *51, 52–53*
 in Filet Mignon, 68–69
 in High-Low Boneless Rib Eye, 62–63,
  64–65
 in High-Low Center-Cut Tenderloin
  (aka Chateaubriand), 66–67
 in Leg of Lamb, 80, *81,* 82

 in Man Steak with Thyme Zinfandel
  Salt, 34, *35, 36,* 37
 in Rib Roast Done Like a Steak, 71–72,
  74–75
 in Roasted Rib Stack with
  Worcestershire Salt, 42–43, *44–45*
 in Smoked Brisket on the Bone with
  Chimichurri Crust, 48–49
 in Thick Pork Chops, Guaranteed Juicy,
  76–78
Boulud, Daniel, 30, 156, 166
broccolini:
 Warm Crunchy Broccolini with
  Prosciutto and Scruffed Croutons,
  192–93
butter, clarified, 149
Butter Baste, 234
 in Clinched Beef Tenderloin, 98–99
 in Clinched Boneless Pork Chops,
  100–101
 in Clinched Chicken Wingettes, 104–5
 in Clinched Double-Wide Loin Lamb
  Chops, 102–3
 in Clinched Strip Steak, 92, *93,* 94
Butter beans:
 Bubbling Bacon Butter Beans, 142–43
Butter Lettuce Salad with Pommery
  Mustard Dressing, Fleur's, 182

cabbage:
 Green Apple, Cabbage, and Caraway
  Slaw, 162–63
capers:
 Potato Cream with Leeks, Capers, and
  Avocado, 152–53
Caponata, Concentrated, 224–25
caramelizing, 2
caraway seeds:
 Green Apple, Cabbage, and Caraway
  Slaw, 162–63
Carbonara Sauce, 148–49
cayenne, 6

Chang, David, 200

charcoal, 86

Charcoal Salt, *47*, 253, *253*, *254–55*

    Lamb in Ash Salt Crust with Charcoal
      Salt, 46–47

Chateaubriand (High-Low Center-Cut
    Tenderloin), 56–57

chicken:

    Chicken Skin Cooked and Crisped
      Under a Brick, 199

    Clinched-and-Planked Chicken Legs,
      124, 126, *127*

    Clinched Chicken Wingettes, 104–5

    Smoked Crack-Back Chicken with
      Lemon, Garlic, and Herbes de
      Provence Baste, 54–55, *56–57*

chile(s):

    Creamed Corn with Chives and Chiles,
      140–41

    Hatch Chile Spackle, 222–23

Chimichurri Baste, 233

    in Smoked Brisket on the Bone with
      Chimichurri Crust, 48–49

chives:

    Creamed Corn with Chives and Chiles,
      140–41

cilantro:

    Mango Cilantro Salad, 164

Classic Southern Baste, 234

    in Roasted Rib Stack with
      Worcestershire Salt, 42–43, *44–45*

    in Smoked Pork Shoulder with Lime
      Coriander Salt, 40–41

classic main courses, 30–57

    Double-Butterflied Leg of Lamb,
      50–51, *51*, *52–53*

    Lamb in Ash Salt Crust with Charcoal
      Salt, 46–47

    Man Steak with Thyme Zinfandel Salt,
      34, *35*, *36*, 37

    Roasted Rib Stack with
      Worcestershire Salt, 42–43, *44–45*

Smoked Brisket on the Bone with
    Chimichurri Crust, 48–49

Smoked Crack-Back Chicken with
    Lemon, Garlic, and Herbes de
    Provence Baste, 54–55, *56–57*

Smoked Pork Shoulder with Lime
    Coriander Salt, 40–41

cleaning the grill, 38, *38–39*

clinched-and-planked main courses,
    106–31

    Clinched-and-Planked Chicken Legs,
      124, 126, *127*

    Clinched-and-Planked Duck Breasts,
      128–29

    Clinched-and-Planked Fish Steaks,
      130–31

    Clinched-and-Planked Game Steaks,
      122–23

    Clinched-and-Planked Lamb Racks,
      118–19, *120–21*

    Clinched-and-Planked Lobster Tails,
      114, *115*

    Clinched-and-Planked Rump Steaks,
      116–17

    Clinched-and-Planked Shrimp, 110, *111*,
      112

clinching, 84–105, *91*

    Clinched Beef Tenderloin, 98–99

    Clinched Boneless Pork Chops, 100–101

    Clinched Chicken Wingettes, 104–5

    Clinched Double-Wide Loin Lamb
      Chops, 102–3

    Clinched Strip Steak, 92, *93*, 94

    cooking "clean on the screen,"
      86, *87*

    "cooking dirty," 84, *85*, 86, *96*

coals, preparing, 90

cooking "clean on the screen," 86, *87*

"cooking dirty," 84, *85*, 86, *96*

corn:

    Creamed Corn with Chives and Chiles,
      140–41

corn (*cont.*)
    Smoked-Corn Flan, 146–47
co-stars, 132
    crispy, fresh, and sprightly (sides),
        158–73
    crispy bits (sides), 194–95
    leaves, lettuces, and greens (sides),
        174–93
    melting, creamy, and comfortable
        (sides), 134–57
Cranberry Spackle, 216–17
cream cheese, as thickener, 140
Creamed Corn with Chives and Chiles,
    140–41
Creamed Spinach with Steeped and
    Smoked Garlic Confit, 154
crispy, fresh, and sprightly (sides), 158–73
    Green Apple, Cabbage, and Caraway
        Slaw, 162–63
    Lemony Asparagus Shavings with
        Goat's-Milk-Curd Dressing, 170–71
    Mango Cilantro Salad, 164
    Peach and Nectarine Salad with
        Slivered Almonds, 168–69
    Pickled Mixed Vegetables, 172
    Pickled Ramps, 166
    Radish and Mint Salad, 167
crispy bits (sides), 194–205
    Chicken Skin Cooked and Crisped
        Under a Brick, 199
    Crispy Moonshine Onion Rings,
        200–201
    Duck-Fat Fries, 198
    Fried Shallot Loaf, 204
    Supercrisp Pork Rinds, 202
croutons:
    Warm Crunchy Broccolini with
        Prosciutto and Scruffed Croutons,
        192–93
crust, 6
cucumber:
    in Mango Cilantro Salad, 164

dancing phase, 12, 15
deep frying, note, 204
dome, *113*
duck:
    Clinched-and-Planked Duck Breasts,
        128–29
    Duck-Fat Fries, 198

eggplant:
    in Concentrated Caponata,
        224–25
elevated grate, 58, 59
endive:
    Belgian Endive Salad with Burnt
        Oranges, Marjoram Dressing, and
        Pomegranate Seeds, 186–87

Filet Mignon, 68–69
finishing items:
    bastes, 226–39
    salts, 240–55
    spackles, 208–25
fish:
    Clinched-and-Planked Fish Steaks,
        130–31
flan:
    Smoked-Corn Flan, 146–47
Fleur's Butter Lettuce Salad with
    Pommery Mustard Dressing, 182
Four Seasons Blend, 5–6, 7
    in Chicken Skin Cooked and Crisped
        Under a Brick, 199
    in Clinched-and-Planked Chicken Legs,
        124, 126, *127*
    in Clinched-and-Planked Duck Breasts,
        128–29
    in Clinched-and-Planked Fish Steaks,
        130–31
    in Clinched-and-Planked Game Steaks,
        122–23
    in Clinched-and-Planked Lamb Racks,
        118–19, *120–21*

in Clinched-and-Planked Lobster
Tails, 114, *115*
in Clinched-and-Planked Rump
Steaks, 116–17
in Clinched Beef Tenderloin,
98–99
in Clinched Boneless Pork Chops,
100–101
in Clinched Chicken Wingettes,
104–5
in Clinched Double-Wide Loin Lamb
Chops, 102–3
in Clinched Strip Steak, 92, *93*, 94
in Double-Butterflied Leg of Lamb,
50–51, *51*, *52–53*
in Filet Mignon, 68–69
in High-Low Boneless Rib Eye, 62–63,
64–65
in High-Low Center-Cut Tenderloin
(aka Chateaubriand), 66–67
in Lamb in Ash Salt Crust with
Charcoal Salt, 46–47, *47*
in Leg of Lamb, 80, *81*, 82
in Man Steak with Thyme Zinfandel
Salt, 34, *35*, *36*, 37
in Rib Roast Done Like a Steak,
71–72, *74–75*
in Roasted Rib Stack with
Worcestershire Salt, 42–43, *44–45*
in Smoked Brisket on the Bone with
Chimichurri Crust, 48–49
in Smoked Crack-Back Chicken with
Lemon, Garlic, and Herbes de
Provence Baste, 54–55, *56–57*
in Smoked Pork Shoulder with Lime
Coriander Salt, 40–41
in Supercrisp Pork Rinds, 202
in Thick Pork Chops, Guaranteed
Juicy, 76–78

Game Steaks, Clinched-and-Planked,
122–23

garlic:
Creamed Spinach with Steeped and
Smoked Garlic Confit, 154
Lemon, Garlic, and Herbes de Provence
Baste, 232
Watercress with Pickled Garlic and
Smoked Anchovies, 184–85
garlic salt, 5

Habanero Syrup, 237
in Thick Pork Chops, Guaranteed Juicy,
76–78
heat, 17–18, 20
dialogue with, 17
hot potato method, 24–25
Mississippi method, 23
pause break in, 22, 24, 38
wood fire, 24
herb basting brush, 8, *9*, 25, 27
herbes de provence:
Lemon, Garlic, and Herbes de Provence
Baste, 232
Smoked Crack-Back Chicken with
Lemon, Garlic, and Herbes de
Provence Baste, 54–55, *56–57*
high-and-slow main courses, 58–83, *67*
Filet Mignon, 68–69
High-Low Boneless Rib Eye, 62–63, *64–65*
High-Low Center-Cut Tenderloin
(aka Chateaubriand), 66–67
Leg of Lamb, 80, *81*, 82
Rib Roast Done Like a Steak, 71–72,
74–75
Thick Pork Chops, Guaranteed Juicy,
76–78
High-Low Boneless Rib Eye, 62–63, *64–65*
High-Low Center-Cut Tenderloin
(aka Chateaubriand), 66–67
hot potato method, 24–25

Jade King Chinese restaurant, Roslyn,
New York, 132

INDEX

Kaminsky, Peter, 186
Keller, Thomas, 240
Kunz, Gray, 166

lamb:
Barnsley chop, 102
Clinched-and-Planked Lamb Racks,
118–19, *120–21*
Clinched Double-Wide Loin Lamb
Chops, 102–3
Double-Butterflied Leg of Lamb,
50–51, *51, 52–53*
English chop, 102
Lamb in Ash Salt Crust with Charcoal
Salt, 46–47
Leg of Lamb, 80, *81*, 82
layering flavor, 15, 17
leaves, lettuces, and greens (sides),
174–93
Arugula Salad with Lemon, Extra
Virgin Olive Oil, and Parmesan
Shavings, 188
Baby Beet Greens and Mâche with
Balsamic and Shaved Pecorino,
190
Belgian Endive Salad with Burnt
Oranges, Marjoram Dressing, and
Pomegranate Seeds, 186–87
Charred Radicchio with Sweet-and-
Sticky Balsamic and Bacon, 178–79,
180–81
Fleur's Butter Lettuce Salad with
Pommery Mustard Dressing, 182
Warm Crunchy Broccolini with
Prosciutto and Scruffed Croutons,
192–93
Watercress with Pickled Garlic and
Smoked Anchovies, 184–85
Le Cirque, New York, New York, 30
leeks:
Potato Cream with Leeks, Capers, and
Avocado, 152–53

lemon(s):
Arugula Salad with Lemon, Extra
Virgin Olive Oil, and Parmesan
Shavings, 188
Lemon, Garlic, and Herbes de Provence
Baste, 232
Lemon Thyme Salt, 246
Lemony Asparagus Shavings with
Goat's-Milk-Curd Dressing,
170–71
Mint, Lemon, and Rosemary Salt, 245
Smoked Crack-Back Chicken with
Lemon, Garlic, and Herbes de
Provence Baste, 54–55, *56–57*
Lemon Oregano Baste, 231
in Double-Butterflied Leg of Lamb,
50–51, *51, 52–53*
in Lamb in Ash Salt Crust with
Charcoal Salt, 46–47
Lima beans:
Bubbling Bacon Butter Beans, 142–43
Lime Coriander Salt, 248
Smoked Pork Shoulder with Lime
Coriander Salt, 40–41
lobster:
Clinched-and-Planked Lobster Tails,
114, *115*

mâche:
Baby Beet Greens and Mâche with
Balsamic and Shaved Pecorino, 190
Maillard reaction, 2, 12
main courses:
classic main courses, 30–57
clinched-and-planked main courses,
106–31
clinching, 84–105
high-and-slow main courses, 58–83
Mallmann, Francis, 186
mango:
Mango Cilantro Salad, 164
Mango Spackle, 214–15

Man Steak with Thyme Zinfandel Salt, 34, *35*, *36*, 37

marjoram:
    Belgian Endive Salad with Burnt Oranges, Marjoram Dressing, and Pomegranate Seeds, 186–87

mascarpone:
    Polenta with Mascarpone and Rosemary, 156

meat:
    basting, 12, 15, 25, *25*
    dancing, 12, 15
    resting, 22, 24
    use of term, 17
    see also Main courses

meat paste, 8

melting, creamy, and comfortable (sides), 134–57
    Bubbling Bacon Butter Beans, 142–43
    Creamed Corn with Chives and Chiles, 140–41
    Creamed Spinach with Steeped and Smoked Garlic Confit, 154
    Melting Potatoes, 150–51
    Mushrooms in Parsley Cream, 138–39
    Polenta with Mascarpone and Rosemary, 156
    Potato Cream with Leeks, Capers, and Avocado, 152–53
    Scruffed Carbonara Potatoes, 148–49
    Smoked-Corn Flan, 146–47
    UKBB (United Kingdom Baked Beans), 144–45

mint:
    Mint, Lemon, and Rosemary Salt, 245
    Radish and Mint Salad, 167

Mississippi method, 23

moonshine:
    Crispy Moonshine Onion Rings, 200–201

Mushrooms in Parsley Cream, 138–39

Nah Trang restaurant, New York, New York, 164

nectarine(s):
    Peach and Nectarine Salad with Slivered Almonds, 168–69

Oliver, Jamie, 8, 178

onion(s):
    Crispy Moonshine Onion Rings, 200–201

oranges:
    Belgian Endive Salad with Burnt Oranges, Marjoram Dressing, and Pomegranate Seeds, 86–87

Parmesan:
    Arugula Salad with Lemon, Extra Virgin Olive Oil, and Parmesan Shavings, 188

parsley:
    Mushrooms in Parsley Cream, 138–39

pause break, 22, 24, 38

Peach and Nectarine Salad with Slivered Almonds, 168–69

pecorino cheese:
    Baby Beet Greens and Mâche with Balsamic and Shaved Pecorino, 190

pepper, black, 5

pepper(s):
    in Habanero Syrup, 237
    in Red Pepper Spackle, 212–13

Perry, William B., 138

Peter Luger's Steak House, Brooklyn, New York, 154

Pickled Mixed Vegetables, 172

Pickled Ramps, 166

pit barbecue method, 58

planking, 106; *see also* clinched-and-planked main courses

Polenta with Mascarpone and Rosemary, 156

pomegranate seeds:
    Belgian Endive Salad with Burnt
       Oranges, Marjoram Dressing, and
       Pomegranate Seeds, 86–87
Pommery Mustard Dressing, 182
pork:
    Clinched Boneless Pork Chops,
       100–101
    Roasted Rib Stack with Worcestershire
       Salt, 42–43, *44–45*
    Smoked Pork Shoulder with Lime
       Coriander Salt, 40–41
    Supercrisp Pork Rinds, 202
    Thick Pork Chops, Guaranteed Juicy,
       76–78
potato(es):
    Duck-Fat Fries, 198
    Melting Potatoes, 150–51
    Potato Cream with Leeks, Capers, and
       Avocado, 152–53
    Scruffed Carbonara Potatoes, 148–49
prosciutto:
    Warm Crunchy Broccolini with Prosciutto
       and Scruffed Croutons, 192–93

radicchio:
    Charred Radicchio with Sweet-and-
       Sticky Balsamic and Bacon, 178–79,
       180–81
Radish and Mint Salad, 167
Ramps, Pickled, 166
resting, 22, 24
Rib Roast Done Like a Steak, 71–72,
    74–75
ribs:
    Roasted Rib Stack with
       Worcestershire Salt, 42–43, *44–45*
rosemary:
    Mint, Lemon, and Rosemary Salt, 245
    Polenta with Mascarpone and
       Rosemary, 156
    Thyme, Rosemary, and Sage Salt, 244

salads:
    Arugula Salad with Lemon, Extra
       Virgin Olive Oil, and Parmesan
       Shavings, 188
    Baby Beet Greens and Mâche with
       Balsamic and Shaved Pecorino, 190
    Belgian Endive Salad with Burnt
       Oranges, Marjoram Dressing, and
       Pomegranate Seeds, 186–87
    Charred Radicchio with Sweet-and-
       Sticky Balsamic and Bacon, 178–79,
       180–81
    Fleur's Butter Lettuce Salad with
       Pommery Mustard Dressing, 182
    Green Apple, Cabbage, and Caraway
       Slaw, 162–63
    Lemony Asparagus Shavings with
       Goat's-Milk-Curd Dressing,
       170–71
    Mango Cilantro Salad, 164
    Peach and Nectarine Salad with
       Slivered Almonds, 168–69
    Pickled Mixed Vegetables, 172
    Pickled Ramps, 166
    Radish and Mint Salad, 167
    Warm Crunchy Broccolini with
       Prosciutto and Scruffed Croutons,
       192–93
    Watercress with Pickled Garlic and
       Smoked Anchovies, 184–85
salt burn, 8
salts, 5, 240–55
    Charcoal Salt, *47*, 253, *253, 254–55*
    Lemon Thyme Salt, 246
    Lime Coriander Salt, 248
    Mint, Lemon, and Rosemary Salt, 245
    Thyme, Rosemary, and Sage Salt, 244
    Thyme Zinfandel Salt, 250
    Wine Vinegar Salt, 251
    Worcestershire Salt, 252
Scruffed Carbonara Potatoes, 148–49
scruffing, 8, 12, *14*

seasoning:
  Four Seasons, 5–6, 7
  like rain, *10–11*
  meat paste, 8
Seven Fires (Mallmann with Kaminsky),
  186
shallot(s):
  Fried Shallot Loaf, 204
shrimp:
  Clinched-and-Planked Shrimp, 110,
  111, 112
sides:
  crispy, fresh, and sprightly, 158–73
  crispy bits, 194–95
  leaves, lettuces, and greens, 174–93
  melting, creamy, and comfortable,
  134–57
sources, 256
Southern Baste, Classic, 234
spackles, 208–25
  Artichoke Spackle, 220–21
  Concentrated Caponata, 224–25
  Cranberry Spackle, 216–17
  Hatch Chile Spackle, 222–23
  Mango Spackle, 214–15
  Red Pepper Spackle, 212–13
  Tomato Spackle, 218–19
spinach:
  Creamed Spinach with Steeped and
  Smoked Garlic Confit, 154
Supercrisp Pork Rinds, 202

tempering, 20, 22, 25
thermometer:
  floating, 20, *21*
  instant-read, 18
thyme:
  Lemon Thyme Salt, 246
Thyme, Rosemary, and Sage Salt, 244
  Double-Butterflied Leg of Lamb,
  50–51, *51, 52–53*

Thyme Zinfandel Salt, 250
  Man Steak with Thyme Zinfandel Salt,
  34, *35, 36,* 37
tomato(es):
  in Bubbling Bacon Butter Beans,
  142–43
  in Concentrated Caponata,
  224–25
  Tomato Spackle, 218–19

UKBB (United Kingdom Baked Beans),
  144–45
umami (fifth taste), 138

vegetables:
  Pickled Mixed Vegetables, 172
  see also crispy, fresh, and sprightly;
  leaves, lettuces, and greens
Very Basic Brine, 238
  Clinched-and-Planked Chicken Legs,
  124, 126, *127*
vodka:
  in Crispy Moonshine Onion Rings,
  200–201

Waltuck, David, 138
Watercress with Pickled Garlic and
  Smoked Anchovies, 184–85
whiskey:
  in Crispy Moonshine Onion Rings,
  200–201
Wine Vinegar Salt, 251
  Smoked Brisket on the Bone with
  Chimichurri Crust, 48–49
wood fire, 24
Worcestershire Salt, 252
  Roasted Rib Stack with Worcestershire
  Salt, 42–43, *44–45*

zinfandel:
  Thyme Zinfandel Salt, 250

CONVERSION CHARTS

Here are rounded-off equivalents between the metric system and the traditional systems that are used in the United States to measure weight and volume.

FRACTIONS	DECIMALS
1/8	.125
1/4	.25
1/3	.33
3/8	.375
1/2	.5
5/8	.625
2/3	.67
3/4	.75
7/8	.875

WEIGHTS

US/UK	METRIC
1/4 oz	7 g
1/2 oz	15 g
1 oz	30 g
2 oz	55 g
3 oz	85 g
4 oz	110 g
5 oz	140 g
6 oz	170 g
7 oz	200 g
8 oz (1/2 lb)	225 g
9 oz	250 g
10 oz	280 g
11 oz	310 g
12 oz	340 g
13 oz	370 g
14 oz	400 g
15 oz	425 g
16 oz (1 lb)	450 g

VOLUME

AMERICAN	IMPERIAL	METRIC
1/4 tsp		1.25 ml
1/2 tsp		2.5 ml
1 tsp		5 ml
1/2 Tbsp (1 1/2 tsp)		7.5 ml
1 Tbsp (3 tsp)		15 ml
1/4 cup (4 Tbsp)	2 fl oz	60 ml
1/3 cup (5 Tbsp)	2 1/2 fl oz	75 ml
1/2 cup (8 Tbsp)	4 fl oz	125 ml
2/3 cup (10 Tbsp)	5 fl oz	150 ml
3/4 cup (12 Tbsp)	6 fl oz	175 ml
1 cup (16 Tbsp)	8 fl oz	250 ml
1 1/4 cups	10 fl oz	300 ml
1 1/2 cups	12 fl oz	350 ml
2 cups (1 pint)	16 fl oz	500 ml
2 1/2 cups	20 fl oz (1 pint)	625 ml
5 cups	40 fl oz (1 qt)	1.25 l

OVEN TEMPERATURES

	°F	°C	GASMARK
Very cool	250–275	130-140	1/2–1
Cool	300	148	2
Warm	325	163	3
Moderate	350	177	4
Moderately hot	375–400	190-204	5–6
Hot	425	218	7
Very hot	450–475	232-245	8–9